"In *Chasing Rainbows and Beyond,* Robert (Bob) Berman provides memoirs of his life, from being a teenage blues band member 'working for the mob' to becoming a highly successful businessman who pursued many different paths during his career. A few years ago, he and his wife, Sondy, his 'true love,' had to face the horror that no parent should ever confront— the diagnosis of amyotrophic lateral sclerosis (ALS) in their first child and daughter, Marjorie Berman Block.

"For most, ALS is a death sentence where the sufferers, over just a few years, lose the capacity to move, swallow, and breathe on their own. ALS has toppled the most muscular and athletic among us and is a relentless foe that afflicts about 35,000 Americans. Following its description by Jean-Martin Charcot in the late nineteenth century, we have advanced only supportive care and now offer enteral nutrition and mechanical ventilation to those wishing to pursue these options. We still have no single, comprehensive understanding of how motor neurons die in ALS and, as Bob Berman suggests, may need to enlarge our image of ALS as being more of a syndrome with many causes that lead to a common, final picture of degenerative weakness. Multiple, large clinical trials of single agents have not revealed efficacy. So perhaps, as he also suggests, we need to change how the FDA manages clinical studies in ALS.

"Bob Berman reveals his dream for raising a billion dollars to solve the mysteries of ALS and develop one or more 'cures.' The recent successes of the 'Ice Bucket Challenge' showed that among other things, thousands of persons with minimal understanding of ALS were willing both to get dunked with ice water and to donate collectively over $100 million for ALS research during the summer of 2014. This reveals to us that people really do care and will show it. They just need to be approached in the right way and given an opportunity to express their compassion. Hopefully, the recent entry of Hollywood into revealing ALS *(The Theory of Everything; You're Not You)* will further educate our fellow citizens about the tragedies of this cruel condition.

"Perhaps what we need is a businessman's approach, leading to a scientific solution, one from someone who understands marketing, who could convince the citizens of Jackson, Mississippi, that they really did need a first-class Chinese restaurant, as described in this book.

"In his book, Bob Berman repeatedly expresses his gratitude to Harvard, where he earned his MBA, and learned and then taught others Harvard's 'case method' of analysis. It will take all of his skills, the tangible and intangible, to succeed in this greatest challenge he and his family have faced. I am confident that Bob Berman—a man who stayed true to his Jewish history and faith in a not-always-welcoming environment, yet embraced the concerns of and treated affectionately his neighbors and fellow citizens (*A House of David in the Land of Jesus*), who has shown himself to have multiple humanitarian goals and is obviously the consummate "people person"—has an excellent chance of reaching his goal.

"As a member of the ALS research community who is trying to understand and overcome this most vicious of all afflictions, I encourage you to read Bob Berman's story. His enthusiasm and passion for success shine through, particularly for his 'Final Four' humanitarian goals that include finding a cure for ALS. As a parent myself, I found his despair over his daughter's diagnosis very meaningful. As a physician-scientist, I cheer his research-oriented fundraising energy. And as a citizen of the world, I wish that we could populate our numbers with many more like him."

—James P. Bennett, Jr. MD, PhD
Bemiss Professor of Neurology, Psychiatry
and Physiology/Biophysics
Director, VCU Parkinson's Disease Center
Virginia Commonwealth University
1217 East Marshall Street
Richmond VA, 23298
www.parkinsons.vcu.edu
www.facebook.com/vcupdcenter
jpbennett@vcu.edu

"Certainly, a billion dollars for ALS research would be wonderful, and possibly transformational."

—Jonathan D. Glass, MD
Professor, Neurology and Pathology
Emory
Director, Emory ALS Clinic
Atlanta, GA 30322
als.emory.edu

"Mr. Berman writes eloquently about his approach to life, problem solving, and his strong belief in helping others. His life story is compelling, engaging, and inspiring! He brings this devotion, positive energy, and approach now to help his daughter and all people with ALS. Working together to fund research and raise awareness, he believes strongly that we can find a cure for ALS. I wholeheartedly agree with Mr. Berman!"

—Merit Cudkowicz, MD
Chief of Neurology, Massachusetts General Hospital
Julieanne Dorn Professor of Neurology
Harvard Medical School
15 Parkman Street ACC 705
Boston, MA 02115

"I had the pleasure of knowing Bob Berman as a Rotary Leader when he was a District Governor in 1999–2000, as well as Sondy, his devoted wife and partner in many of his life's activities. I was especially interested in reading this book because I like knowing more about people such as Bob who have been chosen to hold a leadership role in Rotary International.

"Every person has a story, and those who are leaders in business, civic affairs, philanthropy, and Rotary, who also have a unique family background as in the case of Bob Berman, offer more than enough of a reason for me to learn more about their lives. Bob Berman shares with us anecdotes, experiences, disappointments, successes, and more of what he has learned in the different stages of his life from being a young man to a now proactive senior citizen.

"Because of my own position as a past president of Rotary International, I find of interest how he mentions ideas he has picked up by visiting the booths at twelve International Conventions he has attended. It is admirable that he continues to encourage Rotary clubs and Rotary leaders to support many projects, which he feels will help make this a better world. In a project from one of those booths (which he describes and recommends in this book), I have always looked favorably on the work of Breedlove with dehydrated food. I recall also visiting the plant in Lubbock. My comment at the time was that I wish we could install similar plants and warehouses in different developing countries.

"We also get an opportunity of learning the background on why he will dedicate the rest of his life in supporting what he calls his 'Final 4' Hopes, which involves creating scholarships, helping starving children with dehydrated food, opening a museum of tolerance, and laying out a plan to find a cure for Lou Gehrig's Disease.

"I can assure anyone who reads Bob's new book, *Chasing Rainbows and Beyond,* that they will learn more about what I call Possibilities and Opportunities, which might make a change in their lives.

"Thank you, Bob, for continuing to understand the importance of 'Creating Awareness & Taking Action' in helping to make our world a better world by sharing what you have learned in your lifetime."

Your amigo,

—Frank J. Devlyn
President, 2000–2001, Rotary International
Chairman, 2005–2006, Rotary Foundation

"The world we live in today is very different than the one we grew up in. Society is becoming more 'walled off,' more secluded. That makes books like this, from men like Bob, a true gift. People who devote some or all of their lives to helping others seem to be more and more scarce. If we do not act now, someone reading this book will be affected by ALS before they do something about it. Act now and help change the world. A cure for ALS will most likely be a cure for Alzheimer's and many others associated with the human brain."

—Curt Schilling
  Former American Major League Baseball pitcher who helped lead the Philadelphia Phillies to the World Series in 1993 and won World Series championships in 2001 with the Arizona Diamondbacks and in 2004 and 2007 with the Boston Red Sox. In 2014 he was named an analyst for ESPN's *Sunday Night Baseball.*

"I am in favor of this and any other possibility to eradicate ALS. Your proposed Billion Dollar Plan appears to be a big step in the right direction."

—Archie Manning
  Ole Miss Quarterback, College Football Hall of Fame
  Fourteen years Professional Football primarily with the New Orleans Saints
  Chairman of the Board National Football Foundation and College Hall of Fame

"With this proposal, Bob Berman declares war on ALS. His plan is ambitious and thoughtful, not to mention unprecedented. He calls on the ALS Association to turn his strategy into reality— a great choice."

—Valerie Estess, Director of Research, Project A.L.S.

CHASING RAINBOWS
AND BEYOND

A Spectrum of Life and Hope

CHASING RAINBOWS AND BEYOND

A Spectrum of Life and Hope

ROBERT LEWIS BERMAN

TRIMARK PRESS, INC.
368 SOUTH MILITARY TRAIL
DEERFIELD BEACH, FL 33442
800.889.0693
WWW.TRIMARKPRESS.COM

LIBRARY OF CONGRESS CATALOGING-IN-PUBLICATION DATA

CHASING RAINBOWS AND BEYOND:
A SPECTRUM OF LIFE AND HOPE

ROBERT LEWIS BERMAN

P. CM.

ISBN: 978-1-943401-04-8 · HARDCOVER EDITON
ISBN: 978-1-943401-01-7 · SOFTCOVER EDITION
LIBRARY OF CONGRESS CONTROL NUMBER: 2015947296

J15
10 9 8 7 6 5 4 3 2 1
FIRST EDITION
PRINTED AND BOUND IN THE UNITED STATES OF AMERICA

A PUBLICATION OF TRIMARK PRESS, INC.
368 SOUTH MILITARY TRAIL
DEERFIELD BEACH, FL 33442
800.889.0693
WWW.TRIMARKPRESS.COM

DEDICATION

In my earlier books, the first of which was entitled *More Than Survival*, published by Quail Ridge Press, I dedicated as follows:

This Book is Dedicated to the Children of Mississippi

May it help bring them that something they have never had but have always deserved: an equal opportunity to make their dreams come true.

My second book entitled *A House of David in the Land of Jesus*, published by Pelican Publishing Company, Inc., I dedicated as follows:

This book is dedicated to the God of Abraham, Isaac and Jacob, Of Sarah, Rebecca, Leah and Rachel; The God of all humanity; The Father of us all

This book is dedicated to my one and only true love— My dear wife, Sondy

When it looks like the sun isn't going to shine any more, God put a rainbow in the clouds. Each one of us has the possibility, the responsibility, the probability to be the rainbow in the clouds.

∞ Maya Angelou ∞

CONTENTS

FOREWORD

I actually met the author, who I am privileged to call Bob, as a result of a long-term friendship with his middle daughter, Deborah. Our children went to preschool together over a decade ago. Over the ensuing years, my relationship with the Berman family grew in depth and closeness.

Bob and his wife, Sondy, are certainly as warm and generous and lovely as they appear, however, this "southern-charm exterior" houses two extremely keen intellects accompanied by a great deal of resolve. As the contents of Bob's memoir remind us, he has led a very full life and has encountered a wide cast of characters and business circumstances, some perhaps more unsavory than others. His stories remind us all of the richness of life that is there for the asking when someone is as fearless and imaginative as the author. He also teaches the reader, through example, of the importance of community service. The author never questions his reasons for giving back to society, but rather sees it as an organic part of one's existence, such as many of us view our careers, families, and even hobbies. Bob's dedication to recognizing unmet needs on an international societal level, and his thoughtful means of performing due diligence in an attempt to map out strategic solutions, should serve as a lesson for all of us.

Ultimately my relationship with the author and his wife deepened for all of the wrong reasons—as a result of personal tragedy. As detailed in the book, Bob and Sondy's firstborn child, Marjorie, now an adult mother of three sons, has been diagnosed with amyotrophic lateral sclerosis, also known as

ALS, or more colloquially as "Lou Gehrig's disease." As a person active in biopharmaceutical research and patient support in rare neurological disorders, I was asked to advise the family and assist in navigating the often-treacherous waters of a serious illness that is associated with high morbidity and mortality.

Often when one is suddenly faced with a terrifying diagnosis, there is an element of shock and paralysis that is then followed by a lot of questions that are addressed via research and self-education. Eventually an uneasy combination of hope, denial, and coping emerges. The author and his wife managed to break all of these stereotypes. I recall accompanying them to critical meetings with some of the world's leading ALS physicians and scientists, and watching them participate in what can only be described as a conversation among peers.

This "can-do" attitude, which is always backed up by thorough preparation, a high degree of knowledge, and the unfailingly "steel hand in a velvet glove" approach, has led Bob into unprecedented levels of dialogue with key decision-makers within the research and biotechnology communities. It is not a coincidence that in his book he is able to directly quote executives and scientists with whom he has been communicating on a personal/professional basis. I am confident that these folks have never encountered anyone with the author's unique combination of dedication, imagination, and perseverance. It was only after reading this memoir that I was able to better understand the firm foundation that defines his life's experiences and forward-thinking philosophy.

As an example, the author has taken a practical and clinical view of ALS. Indeed, the solutions that he outlines are a roadmap to solving more than Lou Gehrig's disease. They represent a unique and crystallized vision that allows for action on multiple fronts. It is intuitive and natural to conclude that complex problems cannot be solved with narrow responses. ALS, education, tolerance, and food insecurity are the "Final Four" examples illustrating the author's thoughtful and original perspectives. Again, it is by learning about his earlier years that we are offered a small peek into the experiences and insights that brought him to his current positions and perspectives.

Readers will find this book to be, on the surface, a series of stories and musings that define a full and fascinating life. Many anecdotes offer unique insights into the varied worlds of real estate development, the restaurant business, and even the "Southern mob" among others. However, on deeper reflection, a more serious story emerges. This is the story of a man who uses his abilities, his social conscience, and love for his family to take on many responsibilities, and he has done so with a full heart and a clear mind. It has been a great privilege to have been offered advance access to this remarkable book.

—Rachel Salzman, DVM
Chief Scientific Officer, The Stop ALD Foundation

FOREWORD

The challenge of writing a memoir is daunting. The author must walk a fine line between crafting an excessively boastful account of one's life achievements, or, on the other hand, modestly omitting events that should not be forgotten. There is a lurking temptation also. Considering the deep reservoir of life events that beg for inclusion, the author may yield to that temptation and produce a much too lengthy book that taxes the reader's patience. Bob Berman, an experienced author with two previously published nonfiction books to his credit, skillfully navigates past these hazards and gives the reader a polished product that both inspires and informs.

I have known, respected, and admired Bob Berman since our early childhood. Except for a few years when his family lived in Atlanta, Bob and I literally grew up together. In high school we unhappily shared defeat after defeat as members of the Lexington Hornets football team, an undersized, untalented, and motley crew. Bob was our valiant 135-pound tailback, whose valor and courage far outweighed his lamentable lack of size and speed. The persistence and determination he displayed in each game, however, were harbingers of the success he would achieve later in business.

From the earliest beginnings of our friendship, I realized that Bob possessed an exceptional entrepreneurial talent, a rare ability to visualize opportunities where others see only blank space. The title of this book, *Chasing Rainbows and Beyond*, aptly captures Bob's lifelong pursuit of dreams and aspirations that, with creative imagination and indefatigable persistence, he transformed into reality.

This book, in essence, is an impressive story of American individualism and entrepreneurship. Bob tells this story by stringing together the exciting—often humorous—accounts of his many business successes and his rare failures. The reader laughs—and learns—as Bob recounts his teenage venture into the "minnow-marketing" business and his later exciting and successful adventures as a "big band" leader in certain dark and mysterious dens of iniquity.

But we begin to appreciate the true dimension of Bob's business acumen when he describes the growing tension between himself and the limited-vision executive team of a corporate giant that acquired the family-owned grocer company and chain of supermarkets. After his father's untimely death, Bob inherited the food brokerage business his dad had carefully built over the years. Apparently fearing perceptions of insider favoritism, the corporate executives demanded that Bob sell his interest in the brokerage business. If he refused, the brokerage firm and Bob would suffer catastrophic losses. In a carefully orchestrated—and entirely legal—series of transactions, Bob divested himself of the brokerage stock, selling it to a trusted friend who then employed Bob to run the company. Under Bob's astute leadership, the company grew into one of the largest food brokerages in the South. Years later, Bob re-acquired the stock and resumed ownership and control of his brokerage business.

Bob's out-maneuvering of that staid and unimaginative management team is a genuine David versus Goliath epic, one that is worthy of being included in the casebooks of the Harvard Business School. Although the reader does not learn the detailed management decisions that enabled the growth of the brokerage in subsequent years, we catch a glimpse of Bob's marketing genius in the rollicking description of the "Super Broker Shuffle." Determined to win the huge Nabisco account, Bob wrote a sizzling rap number that he and his sales team performed—

in costume—and posted on YouTube. The originality of the sales pitch undoubtedly played a role in winning the Nabisco account. The video became a hit on YouTube, and portions of it were shown on Jay Leno's *Tonight Show.*

Although Southern Food Brokerage was Bob's principal financial resource, his active entrepreneurial spirit simply could not resist other business opportunities as they arose. This led him into significant real estate development and then to more exotic endeavors as restaurateur, entertainment producer, and television station owner. The reader will convulse with laughter as Bob tells the story of "The Incredible Vanishing Egg Rolls" and relates his unceasing—and often frustrating—efforts to import and placate Chinese chefs who spoke little or no English.

The era of the Golden Dragon Chinese restaurant was followed by the equally turbulent era of the Italian *ristorante,* The Pasta Factory. After several years of managerial misadventures, The Pasta Factory morphed into Victor's, a somewhat more sophisticated establishment featuring a continental cuisine. Ultimately, Bob's sound business acumen prevailed, and he was able to bring his ventures—and misadventures—as restaurateur to a successful financial conclusion.

As the "Age of Restaurants" unfolded, Bob spied gold at the end of another rainbow, one that spelled *Entertainment Producer* in dazzling multi-colored lights. The reader will learn with surprise that Bob's first production, "The Kids Next Door," innocently broke the entertainment color-barrier in Mississippi by featuring the first on-stage multiracial dance troupe. And, thanks to the good karma that hovered faithfully over Bob's business ventures, no critical comment was ever voiced by the media.

His career as a producer peaked with the production of "The Monkees"—a successful money-maker—and reached its nadir when Bob declined to book two then-unknown artists, Glen Campbell and Tom Jones!

Bob's talented wife, Sondy, was President of the Mississippi

Opera Guild when its parent organization, The Mississippi Opera Association, booked and brought to Jackson some of the Met's most notable stars. Among them were Jan Peerce, Robert Merrill, Beverly Sills, and Richard Tucker. Sondy, who is blessed with an incredibly beautiful voice, performed on stage with Richard Tucker in *Aida*.

The reader will share Bob's triumphs and disappointments as he chases a number of other rainbows. His part ownership of a major Jackson television station proved highly profitable— although he had to wait ten years for the pot of gold to spill forth. Other rainbows, including a proposed casino on beautiful Cat Island, two proposed casinos for Jackson, and a major Panera Bread franchise, faded into gray clouds of disappointment.

Chasing Rainbows and Beyond is a delightful read, both entertaining and instructive. But its *raison d'etre* is infinitely more serious. In the four "Hope" chapters, Bob Berman shares with the reader the deep and abiding compassion that lies at the heart of his being. In the first chapter, he lifts up the inspiring concept of a scholarship program that will bring higher education opportunities to the children of Mississippi. If enacted into law, the "Hope Scholarship" would enable any qualifying Mississippi student to obtain a college degree. When Bob was elected District Governor of Rotary International, he adopted as his primary goal the enactment of the Hope Scholarship legislation. Utilizing his business experience and his innate leadership qualities, Bob constructed a workable framework for financing the annual scholarship awards. But alas, the enabling law foundered on the shoals of legislative timidity. The good news is that the idea remains alive. Someday, as the economy improves, Bob's dream will become a living reality.

The next chapter, "Hope for Starving Children," describes Bob's dream of saving the lives of countless starving children in Third World countries. Utilizing the influence and resources of Rotary International, dehydrated food products can be shipped—at much less cost than unprocessed products—to distribution points in Africa and elsewhere. There are many obstacles in the path leading to achievement of Bob's goal, but the idea is alive, and progress is being made toward its fulfillment.

In "Hope for Tolerance," Bob unveils an inspiring plan to create a museum and House of Tolerance on the campus of the University of Mississippi. As he describes its purpose, the center would "relate the great story of tolerance in Lexington (our home town), and tell the story of slavery, the Civil Rights movement, the Holocaust, and the horrific results of intolerance." The concept has yet to be appreciated and adopted by the University, but the dream remains alive. And someday . . .

Bob pours his heart and soul into "Hope for a Cure—ALS (Lou Gehrig's Disease)." The story begins in 2009 when Marjie Berman Block, one of Bob and Sondy's three beautiful daughters, was diagnosed with amyotrophic lateral sclerosis (ALS). Bob has devoted the remainder of his life to a plan to help find a cure for ALS. Through his efforts and the work of family members and friends, significant sums have been raised to fund ALS research. By virtue of sheer courage and determination, Marjie has defied the odds and continues to live and inspire others. Someday, Bob's dream of finding a cure will be realized, and healing grace will embrace the lives of thousands of ALS sufferers and just possibly may include those with other neurological diseases.

And so, dear reader, I invite you to "chase rainbows" with Bob, and then go beyond them with your own dreams.

—Parham Williams, Dean Emeritus
University of Mississippi School of Law

PREFACE

This book began as a memoir of the amazing experiences my wife and I had in two totally different restaurants we founded, one a Chinese restaurant and later, one Italian. As I began to write, however, I recalled a number of other interesting occurrences throughout my life that I had never revealed. As we go through life, especially when reaching my age of eighty-four, we experience many events that we've never talked about. Some are worth revealing, others wither on the vine. Those of mine that have never been told publically but are worthy of being penned, I reveal here in *Chasing Rainbows and Beyond.*

This book contains true stories about a number of my successes and failures. No human realistically goes through life, especially one as long as I've been blessed with, without both success and failure. Anyone who tells you they have had nothing but success during their lifetime and that everything they have touched "turned to gold," is merely "watering" on your leg and telling you it's raining.

Unequivocally, the biggest successes of my life are to have been blessed with my wife, Sondy, our three daughters, Marjie, Debbie, and Sheri, and their wonderful families noted in "About The Author."

As I continued writing this memoir, it developed into much more than a record of my memories. It became a "Motivational Memoir" that I hope could someday be beneficial to society. I decided to conclude my book with four key humanitarian projects of mine: the hope scholarship; hope for starving children; hope for tolerance; and hope for a cure for ALS. As important as I feel these are, they have never reached fruition. If enacted, they could make a real difference. I believe the "embers" within each of these projects still glow, just waiting for someone to fully ignite them by picking up the baton and successfully completing the meaningful race. I think of these four projects as the "rainbows" most worth chasing—with a "pot of gold" for humanity waiting at the end of each. The cure for ALS is currently, and personally, by far the most important to me—and still possible to achieve. I shall remain involved with it until it reaches fruition. My thoughts and action plans for each of these humanitarian rainbows can be found in the final section of the book entitled "Hope."

> The woods are lovely, dark and deep,
> but I have promises to keep,
> and miles to go before I sleep.
> ∞ Robert Frost ∞

ACKNOWLEDGMENTS

Appreciation for initial editing, and throughout the entire writing, goes to my dear wife, Sondy, who implored me to delete almost all mentions of her name in association with most of the successes I have achieved. That I did not do because her intellect and keen perceptions made her a vital part of those achievements.

Appreciation for initial line editing also goes to Gary Davis of Los Angeles. He is one of the brightest, most talented graphic designers in the state of California. He oversees the marketing materials for the Athletics Department at the University of Southern California and was recently awarded similar responsibilities for the New Year's Day Rose Parade and Rose Bowl Game. He also designed the cover of this book, *Chasing Rainbows and Beyond,* and my last nonfiction book, *A House of David in the Land of Jesus.*

Thank you to Candace Johnson of Change It Up Editing and Writing Services for her editing help. Her professionalism was exceptional and a major part of the fine-tuning of my manuscript.

PART I

SIGNIFICANT
EARLY ADVENTURES

1

I Worked for "The Mob"

Beginning in my last year in high school in the rural Mississippi town of Lexington, I started working for "The Mob," and I continued to do so through most of my college days at Ole Miss. Strictly speaking, I did work for the mob, but in a related way through their entertainment complex.

After World War II, in the late 1940s and early 1950s, Mississippi had a plethora of bootleggers and illegal gambling club casinos. In those days of sanctioned prohibition, I formed a ten-piece swing band that played music of the Big Band era, and I was the lead sax. Our theme was "The Sweetest Music This Side of Guy Lombardo" (a take on Lombardo's popular theme, "The Sweetest Music This Side of Heaven"). We called ourselves the DixieKats. Combining the versions of "Deep Purple" popularized by Jimmy Dorsey and Artie Shaw, we arranged our own and made that our theme song, with which we opened and closed each evening's performance. We played music that made people happy and "moved the nation's spirit."

Our dance band had two fantastic pianists. John Yarborough, our primary, was a concert pianist who never missed a note and played each one exactly as it was written in each arrangement. His solo arrangement of "Bumble Boogie" always amazed our audiences. J. B. Robinson, our backup pianist, could never read a note, but he was great at improvising and filling in when needed to enhance the band's sound. He, like Ray Charles, never looked at the keyboard, and didn't need to. The differences between our two pianists were intriguing. They both were terrific in their own personal manner.

The other outstanding musician in our band was the great trumpet player Sonny Hill of Greenwood, Mississippi, who sat in with us when he was not on the road touring with the famous Jimmy Dorsey and Tex Beneke bands. Years after college, after we had long since disbanded, I gave all our orchestrations, bandstands, lighting, and other equipment to Sonny, who was the band director for Jackson Academy in Jackson, Mississippi. One of our popular arrangements was entitled "Down Where the Delta Begins". That's exactly where it all ended. Sadly, the 1979 flood known as the Pearl River Easter Flood and considered to be a 100-year flood washed all the DixieKat material down the Pearl River.

We needed "gigs" to earn money. Thus, as band director, I met with the mobster owners of various illegal casinos, mostly throughout the hill and delta regions of the state, to book engagements for our popular dance band.

Our home base was a club called Rainbow Gardens, located thirteen miles east of Lexington in the small town of Durant, on the main line of the Illinois Central Railroad and Highway 51— at the time the main north-south highway in the state, running from New Orleans to Memphis and northward. The club was located on the final leg of Highway 17, connecting Lexington with Durant.

The club had a large dance hall and bandstand area where we performed on most weekends. The gambling took place in the "back room," where crap tables, roulette wheels, and blackjack tables abounded. Then there was the inner sanctum—the "back office"—where the owner, "Black Jack" Powell, did his business and counted and stored his money—and where we made our deals. They probably let me back there because I was a teenager and they likely considered me harmless.

Black Jack was a tall, handsome, well-groomed man, with slick black hair that was always neatly combed backward from his forehead. He had dark, deep-set eyes that could stare down a tiger. He was always sharply dressed, with well-starched white shirts, cuff links, and brightly colored ties. The back office was also the site of his well-endowed and gorgeous blonde wife. (At least I always addressed her as "Mrs. Powell.") She wore low-cut, sheer black dresses that fell just above the knees. She was an outstanding beauty, and it was difficult for me to keep my eyes off of her, especially when we were alone in the back office and Black Jack was in the casino. However, whenever he was in the office, I never even gave her a second glance—because I didn't want to wind up floating down the Mississippi River. There's a better way to get to New Orleans.

I always treated "Mrs. Powell" as a lady, and I never got within several feet of her, except when she paid me off after each night's gig. At payoff time, Black Jack was usually in the office, and I merely said "Thank you, ma'am." Then I'd hurriedly depart through the back door to divide up the night's take among our other band members who were waiting patiently outside.

Lexington lies on a high hill, just overlooking the vast Mississippi Delta region, which contains some of the most fertile soil on the continent. In fact, a remarkable Irish friend with whom I used to work, once said, "That land is more fertile than two feet up a bull's ass." Now that's really fertile!

Thirty miles to the west of Lexington lays Greenwood, Mississippi, home of Malouff's Club and Casino, where our band also played. The Malouff brothers were sharp and slick no-nonsense businessmen. When I negotiated a gig with them, it was straightforward and quick. I had only two problems, one minor, working with them. One of our trumpet players was from Kosciusko, Mississippi. He came in one evening without his jacket before we went on. They would not let him in the club without it. But they did let him borrow one they had in their office. It may have had a little bloodstain on the sleeve, but we never asked why. We were just glad to have him in the brass section of our band that night. No questions asked.

The only other problem we ever had with the Malouff brothers was when they required us to take more breaks than we were accustomed to doing. We were a dance band that loved to play everything, from the fast tempos of "In The Mood," "Two O'Clock Jump," and "Sweet Georgia Brown," to the slower, more romantic tunes like "Embraceable You," "Smoke Gets in Your Eyes," "Stardust," "Blue Moon," and "I've Got My Love to Keep Me Warm." One of our favorite snappy tunes was known as "Shanty Town," where our entire band stood up and sang it in unison. The crowd loved that! However, the owners wanted more breaks to keep their patrons off the dance floor and in the back rooms for gambling. Of course we accommodated them as they were our "mob bosses," and we were their employees.

Then there was Iggy Collalto and his casino on the outskirts of Indianola, another town in the heart of the Mississippi Delta. The number of patrons he attracted to his gambling complex was amazing. Some of the characters I saw coming in and out of his back-room office appeared somewhat unsavory, but the majority of his customers were well-dressed dudes who came to dance, drink, and gamble away the night. Our band stayed as late as they wanted to dance, and one night it was early in the morning before we wrapped up, got our pay from Iggy, and headed back home.

2

WHAT I HEARD AND SAW IN THE CASINOS STAYED THERE

Everything I overheard, noticed, or saw in the casinos pointed to Black Jack Powell as the undisputed kingpin of the mob in Mississippi and surrounding areas. His people may in fact have used our band as a "front" for their illegal operations so they would appear legitimate. Nevertheless, we considered ourselves fortunate to have those gigs.

From time to time, but more so in our Rainbow Garden headquarters when I was in the back office negotiating more nights or getting our pay, I saw and heard a number of characters coming in and out of the complex. Some looked pretty tough, and their language matched their demeanor. I can guarantee you one thing for certain. Whatever I overheard or witnessed stayed in that room, never to be revealed or discussed with anyone, including band members. There were two primary reasons for my keeping quiet. First, I didn't want to lose a great venue where our band could perform frequently, with reasonably good pay. The other reason was more personal: I definitely didn't want to lose something much more important than our gigs—my life! I didn't want to end up in Black Creek where I had roamed as a boy, or even worse, like Jimmy Hoffa, former president of the Teamsters union. Fortunately, I was never called upon to testify in court since the FBI never knew my whereabouts or even if what I had overheard could possibly be incriminating. Or perhaps all that was only my young, vivid imagination at work.

I'm just thankful I was ignored during my times in the back office when they were speaking directly to associates, either person-to person or over the phone. I imagine they must have felt I was too young to recognize or understand what appeared to me as their undercover dealings. At least, that was what I thought until one evening when I had to wait a considerable time to receive our pay. During that delay, there was a lot of action taking place in the inner sanctum of the back room. Black Jack was not pleased about what had taken place with something or someone in their operation. While waiting, I pretended not to pay any attention to what was happening. I stared at the ceiling, then the floor, then occasionally glanced at Black Jack's gorgeous wife, but not for long! Although I must admit, it was difficult to keep my eyes off of her.

After I finally was paid our minor share of the evening's take, I quickly departed out the back door. During the thirteen-mile drive back to my home, I thought I noticed a car following me on the dark and lonely road between Durant and Lexington. It stayed about fifty to one hundred yards behind me all the way. However, when I increased my speed, it sped up; when I slowed down, it slowed too. It followed me all the way to the entrance to my grandfather's winding driveway up to where we resided in an antebellum home named Faymorcele after my mother Fay and her two brother's Morris and Celian. It always reminded me of Tara in *Gone with the Wind*. Once I made the turn into our private driveway, the car sped off into the darkness, and I never saw it again. I thought the incident was quite unusual, especially at that time of night—we were the only two cars on the road. It did make me uneasy until I was parked at our home, and I was thankful it was no longer following me. Perhaps they only wanted to know where I resided in the unlikely event that the authorities ever brought me into any trial about the events that took place that particular night. Or maybe I was merely paranoid.

Another club where we performed was Grapes's Tourist Camp, a place on Highway 51 on the way to Jackson. We were booked there through one of Black Jack's associates. Numerous "ladies of the night" frequented the small bar area in the club. We would see some of them dancing—extremely closely—with some of the male customers. Later the guys would disappear to the cabins out back with the women they had been dancing with. That was not an unusual occurrence. As long as we were paid, however, we never asked about it; we just assumed that those cabins were for such "tourists" that came along to drink, dance, and whatever. While we obviously never dared to inquire, we definitely were not like "The piano player who was so naive, he played a piano all night in a house of ill repute, and never knew what went on upstairs."

Mob or no mob, I will never forget those experiences. Besides, we loved making music—and making money at the same time. The places we performed in were never raided while we were present, likely because the authorities got their share of the take. As far as we were concerned, the money we received was as "clean as a whistle."

The Rainbow Gardens eventually burned to the ground. Rumors were that it was torched by a competing mob boss or by some local townspeople who wanted to "clean up" the community. However, we knew the real reason. Our music was just too damn HOT!

3

ANOTHER COMMERCIAL VENTURE—THIS ONE FOLLOWED BY IMPLOSION

Just like Tom Sawyer and Huckleberry Finn, the characters in Mark Twain's book *Tom Sawyer*, I used to spend hours on the Mississippi creek banks. Cousin Henry Paris and I seined for minnows on Big Black Creek, which circled the town of Lexington. Beautiful white sand beaches lay along its banks and crystal-clear water ran through its channels, some of which were several feet deep and others only ankle deep. Those shallow areas were where we formed our first commercial venture.

We would use a twenty-foot seine with a fine net and long poles on each side. As we entered the water, we would stretch the seine out across at least half the creek width, from one side to the other. Afterward we would walk downstream until we spotted a school of minnows, and then we would quickly get behind them. Had we approached them from the front and pulled the net upstream, they would have spotted us and swum around the net. Thus we approached them from behind, quickly surrounding them, and circled the net until we had them trapped. We pulled them close to shore, leaving them in the creek water, then we began scooping them up and putting them into large buckets filled with creek water. After we had accumulated about one hundred or so, we would take them to my backyard in Lexington, where our yardman had dug a 15-foot by 4-foot wooden-frame minnow holding pen filled with city water. There we would dump the minnows until fishermen came by to purchase them for bait.

One morning we had accumulated close to 200 minnows when two fishermen came up to purchase a good number for bait. Henry was spending the night with me to assist in the sale. We had stayed up late and did not get to bed until after midnight. At 4:00 A.M. our barber, Mr. Morris, and his friend drove up and honked the horn. We were both awakened but still drowsy. Henry didn't want to move and said "Tell them to come back later." I knew that wouldn't work, so still half asleep, I said, "Don't worry, go back to sleep, and I will handle it." He rolled over and gladly obliged. We were sleeping on what was called the sleeping porch, on the second floor of our spacious home, over the back porch underneath. It was added to the home later and had several windows on each side to catch the breeze, circulate the air, and help cool the room during the hot and humid nights, long before the days of air conditioning.

I went downstairs and met Mr. Morris and his friend at our holding pond. They were meeting some other fishermen later and needed about 100 minnows to fish with all day. We had planned to ask 10 cents per minnow, which would have netted us $10.00 from that sale, and we would still have had half our minnows in the reserve pond. As young boys over sixty years ago, we would have been happy with that for a movie, popcorn, and ice cream, and still have leftover change. However, I was groggy from staying up so late the night before, and when they asked how much, I said $5.00. They said for that price they would take them all—or 200 minnows—and paid me $10.00 (a nickel per minnow). I took their money and staggered back upstairs to bed. That morning when we finally woke up, I gave Henry his $5.00 and I kept $5.00. He said "That was a good sale, and we still have half our minnows left over." I had a puzzled look on my face as I realized all the minnows were gone and that in my stupor I had apparently misquoted the sales price. Then it came to me why our customer took all of them—because I had sold them at half price.

When I confessed to Henry about my mistake in the early hours of the morning when I was half asleep, his jaw dropped. He couldn't believe that after all of our hard work we had made only half of what we were supposed to receive. I replied, "At least you got your $5.00," which did not mollify him at all.

After that, our partnership imploded, never to be restored. That was the last time we ever seined for minnows together or had any business ventures as partners. He later told me that as sleepy as he himself was that morning, had he gone downstairs, there's no telling what he may have sold the minnows for. He may have given them away, since Mr. Morris was always such a good and friendly barber and sometimes gave us a free trim when we didn't have enough money to pay his price.

As life went on, Henry became a highly successful banker, and I had my business successes, but we never did business together again—for minnows or for anything else. However, we did room together at Ole Miss and have always remained close cousins.

4

SMOKING CROSS-VINE ON THE CREEK BANK

The creek bank is where we learned to smoke cross-vine. These are entangled vines that run along the creek banks of Big Black Creek. Once dried in the sun, they become wood-like and can be cut into smaller sections. We would cut them into cigar shapes and light them up. They actually did smoke like a cigar, and would glow at the tip when we dragged in smoke for a puff. However, there were two big differences between cross-vine and real cigars. One favorable difference was that, unlike cigars, cross-vine residue had no odor. The bad part of smoking cross-vine was that it really burned your tongue. That's why we only smoked it for fun and never for long periods of time.

CROSS-VINE OR POT:
THE DANGERS OF EACH

Cross-vine did not give one a "high," and neither was it addictive. Never did it lead to smoking real tobacco products, and surely not marijuana. We only smoked cross-vine to prove we could make our own type of weed to smoke, without having to purchase it, especially when we were too young to buy tobacco anyway.

The biggest danger from smoking cross-vine was not the act of smoking it, but of harvesting it. To reach the cross-vine, we had to traverse the sandy banks of the winding creek, searching for the vines that had dried. While doing that, we had to be extra careful not to step on or near the many cottonmouth water moccasins that lay along the banks, swam the steams, and hung from branches that projected out over the water. They were extremely poisonous. If you were bitten and medical assistance was not available within a relatively short period of time, the bite could be fatal. The color of those reptiles was brownish grey, which allowed them to blend in with the dry foliage near and on the creek banks. And the creeks were full of them, similar to swarms of alligators in Florida, Louisiana, and Georgia swamps, and the crocodiles along the riverbanks in Florida, the Amazon, and South and Central America, and Africa. Some of those moccasins grew as large as four to six inches in width and between six and eight feet long.

One day I was alone on the creek bank, searching for cross-vine. Barefoot and with my khaki pants rolled up above my knees, I walked slowly over the sugar-white sands that sparkled in the sun on bright sunny days. In front of me, about thirty feet away, I saw a large water moccasin curled up, with its head raised up about a foot. To my amazement, it had a bullfrog's head in its jaws. I had never witnessed anything that strange. I froze and then slowly inched forward to take a better look. What I was witnessing was a huge moccasin trying to swallow and digest a large bullfrog, which he had just killed. With the snake's jaws stretched wide open, all that was left showing was the head of the frog projecting from snake's mouth.

Because I didn't believe he could bite me with a frog in his throat, I felt it was safe to move forward to take a closer look. There was no way that reptile could have spit out the frog and come after me while he was attempting to digest it. What I didn't expect to encounter was another large water moccasin nearby, which could have been its mate. It was hanging from a low limb so close by as I walked past it that I could have touched it. When I did notice it, I quickly jumped backward. That aroused the large snake, which promptly dropped from the tree and started after me. The snake and I were at the edge of the creek, about six feet above the water. We both plunged into the creek at the same time. The water level was chest high, and I was not sure if the snake was on top of me or I was on top it. I didn't wait in the water to see. I swam away as fast as I could and crawled back up onto the bank, away from both the moccasin that was devouring the bullfrog and its mate, which had followed me into the water. Those were scary moments, but I managed to get through them. I immediately jumped into my car and forgot all about harvesting any cross-vine that day.

MARIJUANA

President Barrack Obama recently stated publically, "I don't think [marijuana] is more dangerous than alcohol."

If that is true, then with all the problems caused by the consumption of alcohol, why add to it by promoting the use of or legalizing another product that opens the door for more ways to get high or fully inebriated? Both alcohol and marijuana are addictive, but using marijuana can also lead to the use of other far more dangerous and stronger drugs. Additionally, it is my belief that one ounce of alcohol (normally found in a bartender's pour), will not be anywhere as effective as one "reefer" for making one high. Further, it is a lot easier to carry a pack of marijuana around on one's person for a quick smoke, than it is for one to carry around a glass of booze or a bottle for a quick drink—especially when one is driving.

When a person is high on alcohol or marijuana, they have

little or no compunction about their actions and lack a real sense of responsibility. They likely wouldn't know the difference between right and wrong. Even if they did know the difference, they probably wouldn't care. Therefore, why add to the dangers of one drug (alcohol) with another (marijuana) that is easier to carry and conceal?

In an interview by Jake Tapper of CNN, on Tuesday, January 22, 2014, with John Walters, chief operating officer of the Hudson Institute and former drug czar under President George W. Bush, Mr. Walters related the following factual information about the use of marijuana.

In contrast to President Barack Obama's statement that marijuana is no more dangerous than alcohol, Mr. Walters, who has extensive background experience on the subject, takes a diametrically opposite view. He stated that the president apparently has not kept up with the research and facts about marijuana.

Mr. Walters stated that research over the last fifty years shows that marijuana is definitely more dangerous. He said, "It makes you stupid." Sustained use from adolescence onward can cause you to lose IQ points permanently, and may cause other health problems."

According to Mr. Walters, the strength or potency of the marijuana sold today has increased sizably from the 1950s, from containing 3 percent psychoactive ingredients to containing 10 percent—and it can be purchased with up to 20 percent of psychoactive ingredients. That makes marijuana far more potent today than years ago. It definitely can be more dangerous and more addictive; it can cause psychosis, worsening symptoms for people with mental illness, and can even trigger mental illness.

Mr. Walters also stated that other nations that have legalized marijuana—for example, the Netherlands—have begun rethinking its open use. The question is not if one-time or occasional use can hurt you. We have a friend who told us she used to smoke it at parties, and it just made her laugh and even hungry, and she never became hooked on it. She doesn't smoke it today, and neither does her husband, who never used it. That may be so, for those who use it rarely, but even that can be dangerous. The real problem is once people start using it, a significant portion of them do become regular users. Getting high becomes a habit.

Mr. Walters said that it is most important to note that, "Over 50 percent of the people who need treatment for illegal drug use and abuse are marijuana users, more than all other drugs combined"![1] That's a strong condemnation of marijuana.

Even today, now that several states have declared marijuana legal, I do not believe any of my close friends would have even tried it. While I'm not a moralist, and believe marijuana may possibly be proper for medicinal purposes only, it is my hope that the federal government will continue to declare it illegal. Perhaps the fine for its illegal possession or use should be reduced, with no jail sentence for first-time offenders.

On the other hand, regular use of marijuana is another story. For example, students who smoke marijuana regularly likely couldn't care less about their studies or learning; those who drive while on that weed, especially if they become "stoned," could easily run stop lights or run over a child or other innocent human victim, and it simply wouldn't matter to them while they were under the influence. In all probabilities, they would have little or no remorse until they came out of their stupor, and then it would be too late. And consider the effects of the marijuana cookies and candies now being made. How absurd it is to produce marijuana-laced products that not only attract adults, but also children!

California became the first state to legalize medical marijuana use in 1996, when 56 percent of the voters approved Proposition 215.

California Governor Jerry Brown went on NBC's *Meet the Press* on March 2, 2014, where he was interviewed by host

1 http://transcripts.cnn.com/TRANSCRIPTS/1401/22/cg.02.html

David Gregory. While California is one of the most liberal states in this great nation of ours, and a December 2013 Field Poll showed that a majority of Californians—55 percent—approved legalizing marijuana use for the first time since pollsters began tracking opinions on this issue in 1969, Governor Brown cautioned about its possible detrimental effects on both his state and nation.

The governor stated that he is not sure legalizing pot is a good idea in his state because the state could lose its competitive edge if too many people are getting stoned. If pot smoking gains more legitimacy in the nation's most populous state, Brown said, he worries it could have negative ripple effects. He went on to say, "The problem with anything is a certain amount is okay. But there is a tendency to go to extremes." He continued, "And all of a sudden if there's advertising and legitimacy. How many people can get stoned and we still have a great state or a great nation?"

He further stated, "The world's pretty dangerous, very competitive. I think we need to stay alert, if not twenty-four hours a day, then certainly more than some of the potheads might be able to put together."

As Governor Jerry Brown wisely believes, this nation cannot afford to have its population freely smoking marijuana on top of the problems alcohol causes to society.

According to a study published Tuesday, April 15, 2014, in the *Journal of Neuroscience* and partially funded by the Office of National Drug Control Policy, using marijuana a few times a week is enough to physically alter critical brain structures.

> "Just casual use appears to create changes in the brain in areas you don't want to change," said Hans Breiter, a psychiatrist and mathematician at the Northwestern University Feinberg School of Medicine in Chicago. . . .

In his study, done in collaboration with researchers at Harvard University, scientists looked at the brains of 20 relatively light marijuana users [defined as fewer than four times a week] and 20 people who did not use it at all. All forty were college students in the Boston area.

The study found volume, shape, and density changes in two crucial brain areas—the *nucleus accumbens* and the *amygdala*—involved with emotion and motivation and some types of mental illness. . . . The more marijuana the students smoked, the more their brains differed from nonusers, the study found.[2]

On April 30, 2014, Michele M. Leonhart, Administrator of the Drug Enforcement Administration (DEA), testified before the United States Senate's Committee On the Judiciary in a hearing on oversight of the Drug Enforcement Administration. Some of her testimony, supported by statistical facts, is as follows:

Since 2006, we have seen important decreases in the number of past month users, aged 12 and older of cocaine (from 1.0 percent to 0.6 percent, or roughly a million fewer persons).2 Statistics like these demonstrate that through a balanced drug control strategy, one that the DEA has a balanced drug control strategy, one that includes strong enforcement, education, prevention, and treatment components. . . .

In addition, approximately 19.8 million Americans have used marijuana in the past month, more than on any other illicit drug. Currently, marijuana is the most widely available and commonly abused illicit drug in the United States. In 2012

2 http://www.usatoday.com/story/news/nation/2014/04/15/marijuana-brain-changes/7749309/

51

alone, nearly 32 million people ages twelve and older reported using the drug within the past year, and in 2013 one out of every fifteen high school seniors was a near-daily marijuana user. A major study published in the Proceedings of the National Academy of Sciences in August 2012, found that long-term marijuana use started in the teen years has a negative effect on intellectual function in adulthood; the more persistent the person's dependence on marijuana, the more significant the impairment. Heavy marijuana users also reported that the drug impaired several important measures of health and quality of life, including physical and mental health, cognitive abilities, social life, and career status. . . . These statistics help describe the effects of marijuana and the health and safety implications on the users themselves, their families, and our communities. . . .

In 2006, the FDA noted that "there is currently sound evidence that smoked marijuana is harmful," and "that no sound scientific studies support medical use of marijuana for treatment in the United states, and no animal or human data support the safety or efficacy of marijuana for general medical use. . . . The National Institute on Drug Abuse and other components of the National Institutes of Health are conducting research to determine the possible role that active chemicals in marijuana, like THC, CBD, or other cannabinoids may play in treating autoimmune diseases, cancer, inflammation, pain, seizures, substance use disorders, and other psychiatric disorders. . . . The DEA supports these scientific research efforts . . . [3]

In November 2013, the American Medical Association amended their position on cannabis, stating that "(1) cannabis

---

3 http://www.justice.gov/dea/pr/speeches-testimony/2014t/091814t.pdf

is a dangerous drug and as such is a public health concern; (2) sale of cannabis should not be legalized; (3) public health–based strategies, rather than incarceration, should be utilized in the handling of individuals possessing cannabis for personal use; and (4) that additional research should be encouraged."[4]

The American Academy of Child and Adolescent Psychiatry stated, "Adolescents are especially vulnerable to the many adverse development, cognitive, medical, psychiatric, and addictive effects of marijuana."[5]

The DEA's May 2014 report, *Dangers and Consequences of Marijuana Abuse,* states, "Increasingly, the international community is joining the United States in recognizing the fallacy of arguments claiming marijuana use is a harmless activity with no consequences to others."[6]

Antonia Maria Costa, former Executive Director of the United Nations Office on Drugs and Crime, wrote in an article published in *The Independent on Sunday:*

> Evidence of the damage to mental health caused by cannabis use—from loss of concentration to paranoia, aggressiveness, and outright psychosis—is mounting and cannot be ignored. Emergency-room admissions involving cannabis use are rising, as is demand for rehabilitation treatment. . . . It is time to explode the myth of cannabis as a 'soft' drug.[7]
>
> A National Institute on Drug Abuse report stated:
> "We are increasingly concerned that regular or daily use of marijuana is robbing many young people of their potential to achieve and excel in school or other aspects of life," said National Institute on Drug Abuse

---

4 http://www.justice.gov/dea/docs/dangers-consequences-marijuana-abuse.pdf
5 http://www.aacap.org/AACAP/Policy_Statements/2012/AACAP_Medical_ Marijuana_Policy_Statement.aspx
6 http://www.justice.gov/dea/docs/dangers-consequences-marijuana-abuse.pdf
7 http://www.independent.co.uk/news/uk/crime/antonio-maria-costa-cannabis-call-it-anything-but-soft-441735.html

(NIDA) Director Nora D. l. Volkow, MD. "THC, a key ingredient in marijuana, alters the ability of the hippocampus, a brain area related to learning and memory, to communicate effectively with other brain regions. In addition, we know from recent research that marijuana use that begins during adolescence can lower IQ and impair other measures of mental function into adulthood. . . .We should also point out that marijuana use that begins in adolescence increases the risk [adolescents] will become addicted to the drug," said Volkow. "The risk of addiction goes from about 1 in 11 overall to about 1 in 6 for those who start using in their teens, and even higher among daily smokers."[8]

Dr. David Sack, board-certified in psychiatry, addiction psychiatry, and addiction medicine, wrote in a June 27, 2014, *Los Angeles Times* op-ed:

Marijuana sets up kids for failure. We give children one overriding task: to learn. Introducing a substance that slows reaction time, distorts judgment, and interferes with memory short-circuits that task. In addition, the younger kids are when they try marijuana, the more likely they are to become addicted (yes, marijuana can be addictive) and the more likely they are to go on to use other drugs. One analysis by Columbia University researchers found that teens who had used marijuana at least once in the previous 30 days were almost 26 times more likely than those who never used marijuana to try other drugs such as cocaine, heroin, methamphetamines, LSD or Ecstasy.[9]

8 http://www.drugabuse.gov/news-events/news-releases/2012/12/regular-marijuana-use-by-teens-continues-to-be-concern
9 http://www.latimes.com/opinion/op-ed/la-oe-sack-marijuana-children-dangers-20140627-story.html

Dr. Sack is chief executive of Elements Behavioral Health, a network of mental health and addiction treatment centers that includes adolescent and young adult rehab programs.

Legalization of marijuana, especially for recreational use, irrespective of when it begins, will come at the expense of our children and public safety. It will create dependency and treatment issues, and will open the door to use of other drugs, impaired health, delinquent behavior, and drugged drivers.

According to a July 28, 2014, article in "The Nation" section of the *Los Angeles Times* that quoted a *New Yorker* interview published in January 2014, President Obama stated, "I don't think it (marijuana) is more dangerous than alcohol," which I firmly believe is an erroneous belief. The article continued, "But he worried legalizing marijuana would create a slippery slope for legalizing more dangerous drugs."

That same article stated, "In Gallup's most recent survey on the issue, in 2013, 58% of respondents said marijuana should be legalized. . . ." However, I believe it is important to note that the Gallup survey it did not question whether the respondents were specifically referring to "medicinal" use (with which I concur), or "recreational" use (which I vehemently oppose), or both. That differentiation could considerably alter the significance of that particular survey.

Finally, that same *Los Angeles Times* article quoted what Colorado's Governor John Hickenlooper stated in June 2014. His state was the first to fully legalize marijuana. His words were, "I've urged all the governors to go cautiously on this because I think there are risks that we're only just beginning to understand. But this is going to be one of the great social experiments of the 21st century." In the meantime, such an experiment could literally risk ruining a lot of lives, either directly from the use of the drug, or the results of its usage on others.

To reiterate, there are more than enough problems with alcohol abuse and those driving under its influence. Why add to it by legalizing marijuana, other than strict control for medicinal purposes if that in itself is truly proven safe and of benefit to those in dire health?!

5

HUNTING FOR SPORT; HUNTING FOR PEOPLE

My father, Joe Berman, was a gregarious man who died far too soon in a commercial airliner plane crash. Prior to World War II in 1940, he was in the Army Reserve as a captain and saw the oncoming storm. As a patriot and man who loved his country and was thankful for its advantages and freedoms—especially as a man dedicated to his Jewish faith— he volunteered early and rose to the rank of full colonel. The military offered him the rank of general if he remained in the service as a career after the war's end. However, his love of family was greater than his love for a military career, so he chose to return home to his wife, Fay, and two children, my sister, Joan, and me.

He was a lieutenant in the infantry during World War I, but as an attorney was assigned to the Judge Advocate General's department when he re-upped for World War II. After serving the first part of the war at the Central Army Command in Atlanta, he asked for overseas duty. He was shipped out to the Pacific and Hawaii, on the way to Okinawa, where the fighting continued for control of that strategic island. It was to be a staging area for the attack on Japan if that eventuality ever came about. Fortunately, before that happened, President Harry Truman made one of the most courageous and strategic decisions to end the war—the dropping of two atomic bombs on Japan.

Afterward my father was reassigned to Korea, as a judge of the Japanese War Criminal trials. It was during that time that he toured a Japanese arsenal and found a beautiful Belgian-made twelve-gauge double-barreled shotgun. He brought that gun home to me, and I always treasured it and hunted with it frequently. My cousin Henry Paris and close friend John Murrell McRae accompanied me on many a hunt for quail and dove. We used to walk for miles through sage grass country near Franklin, Mississippi, home of my good friend Julian B. Watson. We deftly followed our hunting dogs, one in particular by the name of Ric. He was a handsome black and white English setter with great range. He knew just when to pause and freeze when he found a covey of quail. We would slowly move forward. When he noted that, he would charge forth, and that's when the covey of quail would take off. I can still hear the flutter of their wings as they rose from their ground cover, and I can make that sound myself, even today. We had other hunting dogs also—pointers and red Irish setters—but Ric was always the one that most frequently scented or saw the birds, either nesting or running on the ground.

I will never forget one hunting expedition—it's still as clear as day. We were hunting quail when a rabbit ran out of the brush and right past the feet of John McRae. As soon as the rabbit got a few feet in front of John, I quickly lowered my shotgun and blasted him. The expression on John's face was one of shock to have seen a rabbit killed so close to him. My actions were instantaneous, and had I thought more about it, I would have never taken that shot. But I was a good shot with the twelve-gauge and seldom missed. After that happened, John would continue to accompany me hunting, but for some reason, he always walked behind me, while the rest of us followed right behind the dogs.

We also hunted dove when they were in season, and waited in the fields for them to circle in droves in order to pick one or more out. Ric and the other dogs were also great retrievers and would pick them up and bring them to us after we had felled them. Some were wounded but still alive, so we mercifully killed them by striking their heads with the butts of our guns or wringing their necks to put them out of their misery.

Most of the brown and tan sage grass is now gone on the large acreage of land owned by Julian Watson in Franklin, where we used to hunt. It is now a forest covered with miles of pine trees, planted as his investment in the future. He is the pine tree farmer in the state of Mississippi. Today, whatever few quail remain now strangely roost in his trees instead in their natural habitat on the ground, hidden among the former sage grass–covered hills and valleys.

Our family had a wonderful cook named Ruth. Prior to our hunts, she would bake a snack to take with us called "cracklin' bread." It was corn bread with pork rinds cooked into it to give it that extra taste, which made it absolutely delicious. On cold days during especially long hunts, it gave us that extra energy to continue until we had bagged our legal limits.

I used my trusty single-barreled .22 caliber rifle to hunt bullfrogs along the lake banks. We hunted them at night, and while we could hear them croak loudly, the main way we located them was by shining a strong searchlight in the direction from which the croaking was emanating. We could then see their big eyes gleaming in the light. The light blinded them, and we could pick them off—aiming right between those gleaming eyes. We used a hollow point cartridge because once it hit its target, it exploded, killing the frog instantly. (That experience helped me later in life when I was on the rifle range in the army.) Once the frogs were hit, they sunk into beneath the water lily pads. We would wade out to get them, reaching down under the water, hoping that we would not come up with a dangerous cottonmouth water moccasin instead.

Frog legs are delicious and even more tasty than chicken. The only part of the bullfrog worth eating is its legs. However, after preparing them for the skillet, but before cooking, you needed to take the tendon out of the legs; otherwise they will literally jump in the pan when they begin to cook. Most people did not like to see that as it spoiled their appetite (although the meat tasted the same). I also liked dining on quail, a real treat to me as it was all white meat and tasted like chicken breast but more tender. I never cared to eat dove, though, as it was dark meat and tasted like liver.

I enjoyed hunting with my shotgun and .22 rifle. I did not need any other type of gun, even when hunting large red fox squirrel. They were much larger than the common grey squirrels seen around the yards in most of the country. We had to go deeper into the woods to find them, looking out for their colorful, bushy red tails. Just as we did with the bullfrogs, we only ate the legs of the squirrels—and that was only in a stew.

THE EVIL HUNTER: HUNTING FOR PEOPLE

Despite what many say is our right under the second amendment to the United States Constitution, during my hunting days I never even envisioned needing or utilizing automatic and semiautomatic rifles and pistols with clips that fire a multitude of shots without the need to reload—guns such as the AK-47.

While serving in the military, I witnessed the destructive power of these weapons of war, which are used to destroy a massive number of the enemy as quickly as possible. The only thing they are good for hunting is people, and for killing many of those people at one time. For gun practice, try something else, as we did in the military. We used small-clip M1 rifles. If anyone needs an AK-47 or similar weapon to hunt deer or other large game, he or she is not a true sportsman or sportswoman.

The second amendment was written during revolutionary days when each home needed a weapon to protect them against foreign enemies, militias, insurrections, or unlawful individuals where no army or law enforcement was readily available. Today, a pistol, rifle, an automatic shotgun or gun with clips that can fire up to eight rounds before reloading should be more than enough to protect one's home or loved ones. Any other protection should be left up to our local and state police, our sheriffs' offices, the United States Army (including its National Guard and commandos), Navy Seals, Marines, and Air Force.

The United States has by far the highest per capita rate of firearm-related murders of all developed countries. The latest United Nations' numbers are as follows:

United States:	9,960	1 in 31,000
Canada:	173	1 in 125,000
Spain:	90	1 in 500,000
Germany:	158	1 in 500,000
Australia:	30	1 in 1,000,000
England and Wales:	41	1 in 1,000,000
Japan:	11	1 in more than 1,000,000

Weekly shootings occur in malls, theaters, restaurants, workplaces, and even worse, in schools, where our most cherished possessions are not safe anymore. These shootings that murder innocent people are becoming commonplace in our society. Something drastic needs to be done to put an end to this nonsensical and deadly violence that maims and kills and literally tears apart families—the bedrock of civilization. When a child, a mother, a father, grandparents, teachers, and friends are murdered without cause, they can never be replaced in the minds and hearts of their loved ones, who lost them without any cause, rhyme, or reason.

Our country, the United States of America, is the greatest of all nations on this small planet that we all inhabit. Our freedoms are the greatest, yet there is a limit to freedom. One does not have the freedom to needlessly kill, yet that is exactly what is transpiring most every day, almost to the point of being out of control.

According to the Brady Campaign to Prevent Gun Violence, the U.S. firearm homicide rate is twenty times higher than the combined rates of twenty-two countries that are our peers in wealth and population. American children die by guns eleven times as often as children in other high-income countries. In one year, more than 100,000 people in America are shot in murders, assaults, suicides and suicide attempts, accidents, or by police intervention, including 18,000 children and teens. The lifetime medical cost for all gun violence victims in the United States is estimated at $2.3 billion, with almost half the cost borne by U.S. taxpayers.

It has been said that "guns don't kill people, people do." But of course, if so many guns, especially with large clips, were not available, then people could not use them to kill others.

Our country is better than this! There must be a way to stop this terrible violence and begin to protect our citizens, our families, and our friends.

It must begin with our republican form of democracy. Winston Churchill, perhaps the greatest statesman of all time, once said, "Democracy is the worst form of government in all the world—except for all the others." That being true, we need to use our form of government to begin to protect our society. That starts with the legislative branch that makes the laws, the United States Congress. Yet because of partisan politics and money from lobbyist (that is, donations to congressmen or women) nothing is done to achieve that purpose.

The very first step toward gun-control reform should be the easiest. National polls have shown that 90 percent of our public approve of universal background checks for those who want to purchase a gun of any kind. This would include guns sold online and at gun shows. Currently, our country's background-check system only applies to about 60 percent of gun sales. There are always loopholes for criminals and others who want to skirt the law and acquire guns. Nevertheless, every life that can be saved by tightening restrictions about who can purchase a gun should be worth the effort of legislation and be mandatory on the part of our Congress. Yet pathetically, even this legislation could not be passed. The Senate did move to consider an amendment that would have expanded background checks. But the amendment failed to win the necessary sixty votes to proceed to a final vote.

Gabrielle Giffords, the former Arizona congresswoman who was shot in the head while meeting with constituents on January 8, 2011, wrote the following op-ed for the *New York Times* on April 18, 2013, the day after the Senate vote failed:

> Some of the senators who voted against the background-check amendments have met with grieving parents whose children were murdered at Sandy Hook, in Newtown. Some of the senators who voted no have also looked into my eyes as I talked about my experience being shot in the head at point-blank range in suburban Tucson two years ago, and expressed sympathy for the eighteen other people shot besides me, six of whom died (including a little girl admirer of Gabrielle). These senators have heard from their constituents—who polls show overwhelmingly favored expanding background checks. And still these senators decided to do nothing. Shame on them.[10]

I say "ditto" to the last three words of her op-ed.

The National Rifle Association (NRA) has a stranglehold on most of these senators and others in Congress who do not

---

10 http://www.nytimes.com/2013/04/18/opinion/a-senate-in-the-gun-lobbys-grip.html?_r=0

support what the great majority of Americans want—universal gun background checks. That shows what money ("the root of all evil") can do. Those pusillanimous individuals in Congress are so afraid of losing financial support and votes from the well-financed and influential NRA that they have been willing to vote against their own constituents and conscience while knowing what is really best for our country and its inhabitants. Had any of them ever lost a child or another dear one to needless gun violence, it is my belief that in their grief their vote would have been different.

What will it take to break the chains that bind so many of our congressmen and congresswomen to the NRA? It will take just one simple word, and that is COURAGE—the same courage that was exhibited by Mississippi's U.S. Senator L. Q. C. Lamar, who put his convictions of righteousness, honor, and duty to his country above local politics and petty sectionalism at the risk of his own political career. His speech on the U.S. Senate floor in 1878 in opposition to the inflationary Bland Silver Bill, despite express instructions from the Mississippi legislature to support it, was an intrepid act. His stirring words, "Today I must be true or false . . ." put personal convictions of what was best for the country ahead of the wishes of his constituents. And in doing so, he eventually won the respect and admiration of his fellow Mississippians and the entire nation. For further reference about L.Q.C. Lamar, I refer one to John F. Kennedy's book *Profiles in Courage,* where he wrote admiringly and selectively about this distinguished Mississippian.

Stronger laws limiting the availability of guns for the mentally ill, as well as for those convicted of a crime, are needed through these expanded background checks; additionally, better identification of the mentally ill is needed.

Finally, this country also needs to ban high-volume ammunition clips and assault weapons for everyone other than our military and police personnel. The only thing they are good for is to kill a massive number of humans in the least amount of time. In war? Yes! In peace? No!

Recreational target practice can be achieved by utilizing the same procedure used at a military firing range—one semiautomatic round at a time at a fixed target—or at the most, a few more rounds at a time, even at moving targets, i.e., skeet shooting. But surely not the tommy gun or machine gun approach!

These gun reform actions, over time, will help eliminate a huge amount of unnecessary and innocent suffering and grief in our society.

6

MY TIME IN SOLITARY CONFINEMENT

When I graduated from the University of Mississippi (better known as "Ole Miss"), it was still during the days of prohibition in Mississippi. Unlike today, casino gambling and the sale of liquor were illegal. By then our band had disbanded.

Shortly after graduation, I was celebrating with fellow graduates on the roof of the famous Peabody Hotel in Memphis, Tennessee. The next evening, I had a date with a very attractive girl in Indianola, Mississippi. I had been asked by my uncles, Morris and Celian Lewis, to go by Abe Lewis's liquor store and pick up a case of Seagram's Canadian Club and a case of Cutty Sark Scotch and then bring them with me on my trip back to Indianola. (Liquor sales were legal in Tennessee.) Another cousin, Cecil Herrman, was manager of that liquor store and always gave us first-class service. Anytime our family purchased in case lots, owner Abe Lewis (no relation to our Lewis family) gave us a discounted price. Cecil had those two cases placed securely in the trunk of my father's new blue Cadillac, which he had allowed me to drive home from Memphis, with a stopover in the Delta town of Indianola.

After gulping down a Virgin Mary (never drink while driving), and a big order of barbeque ribs at the well-known Rendezvous barbecue restaurant across from the Peabody, I began my trek south. It was normally about a two-hour trip, but since it was the Fourth of July, traffic could be somewhat heavier. Therefore, I decided to leave as soon as I could after lunch on that bright and sunny holiday.

On the way down U.S. Highway 61, known as the "Blues Highway," the new Cadillac was such a smooth-riding machine that it was too easy to let the speed rapidly increase. Halfway to my destination, as I entered the Mississippi Delta, I was speeding through the small Mississippi town of Tunica. Known as "Sugar Ditch," the town was so poor that it had the highest unemployment rate in the state and one of the highest in the country. Today things are different. Tunica abounds in casinos (it's Mississippi's second largest gaming market), and has one of the highest employment rates in the country.

I didn't realize it, but I had been breezing along approaching 90 miles per hour. All of a sudden I heard a siren and looked in my rearview mirror to see a Mississippi highway patrol car with flashing lights. I pulled over to the side of the road and waited for the patrolman to approach my car. Realizing that the first thing I would be asked for was my driver's license, I had it ready to hand him. He asked me if I knew what speed I was doing, and I had no real clue. When told it was over 90 miles per hour, I frankly was surprised, especially since I was in the center of town (where the highway ran through).

Then I told the officer I needed to be in Indianola early that evening, and I couldn't afford to be late. So I asked, "Will you write me a ticket now, so I can move on?" That likely really irked the officer. His reply was, "You just get into my car, and my fellow officer will drive yours and follow us to the courthouse, where you will be tried and sentenced."

After arriving at the county courthouse, I was told that the judge was at his home watching a baseball game, and would be in later. I said, "Fine, I'll just sit down in the courtroom and wait for him." The patrolman replied, "No you won't. Just follow me over to the jail." Once I entered the jail, I said, " I'll just sit down here and wait for the judge." The officer said, "No you will not. Empty your pockets and put the contents in this bag." I asked him what was that all about, and was astounded when he told me I was going up the stairs to be put behind bars and held until the judge arrived to try me.

On the way up the stairs with the jailer right behind me, I yelled to the patrolman, "I have a right to make a phone call!" His reply: "You're not calling anyone." As I was yelling back to him about my constitutional rights, I was shoved into a holding cell, and the cell door was locked behind me. That was the first time I had ever been jailed behind bars, but that would not be the last or worst of it. At least there I could look down at the entrance to the jail. There was more to come.

There was a scraggly and elderly old man in the cell next to me. He heard me continuing to shout through the bars that I had a right to a phone call. He looked through the side bars separating our adjacent cells and asked, "Do you want me to get their attention?" I answered "Absolutely!" He then took his tin cup and started rattling it against the cell bars and yelling unintelligible words.

The jailer ran up the stairs, looked directly into my eyes, and said, "My wife is busy cooking supper for our family and you prisoners, and if you don't shut him up, I'm going to put you in solitary confinement."

My answer was, "I can't control him. He's crazy." My jailer was true to his threat and did exactly what he said he would. He unlocked my cell, handcuffed me, and pulled me forward deep inside the jail, where I was shoved into a dark, small, eight-foot by six-foot concrete cell with no windows and a small bench to sit on. At least he mercifully removed the handcuffs, which had begun cutting into my wrist. I mumbled to myself, "I guess it could be worse, they could have shot me." So I just kept quiet from then on; besides, in that cell, no one would have heard me.

I sat hunched over in that dank cell for another three hours before a trustee came in carrying a tin tray of food with my prisoner's supper, which included turnip greens, corn bread, black-eyed peas, and a slice of ham. While I love turnip greens and black-eyed peas, I was in no mood to eat, especially from that prison tray, which actually looked dirty to me. A tin cup of water was also put in my cell, but I wouldn't drink a drop from it.

Before the trustee departed to the main part of the jail (I was apparently the only one being held in solitary confinement), I called him over, gave him a $5 bill, and said that if he would call one of my uncles in Indianola and tell them to get me out of there, I would give him another $5 bill when they came to get me. I really should have torn it in half and offered to give him the other half plus one more if he helped "spring" me.

That never occurred to me, and he never returned. I did see him once more as I was departing late that afternoon. He was picking cotton in a nearby field. As I drove by, he yelled, "How about giving me that sport coat you are wearing?" You can imagine my last words to him, which I yelled from my car window.

About 5:30 that same afternoon, the jailer came to get me and escort me over to the courthouse, where the judge was holding court. The judge presented me with a bill for $48, which covered my fine and court cost of $45—and $3 for the meal. I said to the judge, "I have never been treated like that in all my life!" He replied "Son, if you don't shut up and pay your fine now, you will end up under the jail." I said no more, but I didn't have $48 on me. I did have a friend from Ole Miss known as "Red" White, a really fine chap who I had known and befriended. He was a few grades below me, but we were friendly classmates and had a couple of classes together. The judge allowed me to put in a call to him. He was out, but I recalled his father was an attorney in Tunica, so I called him. After identifying myself, he kindly agreed to endorse my check and I was on my way to Indianola. In departing he asked me how fast was I going, and I told him they said 90 miles per hour. He said I was lucky I was both safe and had only been fined $48. He cautioned me to slow down, the same as I would have done to my children or grandchildren.

I was lucky on one more count as well: My car had been sitting out next to the jail and courthouse, with the keys in it, and none of the authorities ever opened and searched the trunk—where they would have discovered those two cases of liquor, illegally transported across state lines. Had they done so, they could have confiscated my dad's car, and I could have spent prison time in the state penitentiary in Parchman. I was fortunate to get out of there when I did, even $48 poorer. I did make my date on time.

As Paul Harvey, the famous radio commentator, used to say—"Now for the rest of the story."

After the episode, my father, Joe Berman, called the judge who'd fined me to complain about the shabby treatment they gave me that July 4th in Tunica. The judge responded: "We give all those whippersnappers speeding through here from Memphis a rough time." My father informed him that I was from Mississippi and didn't deserve to be treated that way. He didn't take the argument any further because I had, prior to his call, told a number of my friends about having two cases of liquor in my trunk and that the authorities never discovered them. Had he made a case about my mistreatment, and it was discovered I had transported liquor illegally—even harmlessly (I thought), for my uncles—into a dry state, it could have made my situation much worse. Therefore my father told me to "drop it," and in the future, "Quit talking so much, and definitely stop speeding!"

That wasn't the end of the story. LeRoy Paris, father of my cousin Henry Paris, had roomed with my dad at the University of Georgia. As previously stated, Henry and I had been roommates at Ole Miss. LeRoy also called Tunica about my incident. He spoke with the highway patrolman who arrested me, as he personally knew him. LeRoy asked, "Why were you so rough on my young cousin when you arrested him for speeding on July 4th? Why didn't you just give him a ticket and let him be on his way, as normally done?" The officer responded, "Mr. Paris, when that young cousin of yours left the courtroom, he took off speeding just as fast as when I had first stopped him!" No more was said.

7

MY DEATH IN THE MILITARY

In ROTC at Ole Miss, I was initially assigned to the quartermaster. However, my father, Colonel Joseph E. Berman, had served in the infantry during World War I, and later as Judge Advocate General (JAG) during World War II, where he was on Okinawa and later served as a judge for Japanese war criminal trials in Korea. I wanted to be where the action was too, so I applied for a transfer to the infantry and was accepted.

After graduating from a three-month Basic Infantry Officers Course at Fort Benning, Georgia, most of the new officers in almost every class were assigned to units that were destined to be sent to Korea during the Korean conflict. My class was one of the few that were assigned elsewhere. I was assigned to the 10th Infantry Division, as a platoon leader. Our division was held in reserve, combat ready, but never sent to Korea.

One early morning, as day broke, my platoon was on a simulated training mission (of which we had many), and we were assigned to take a hill occupied by enemy troops. As I led them in attack formation across a road and down a valley toward the target, I decided to take my platoon sergeant and climb a hilltop to our right to reconnoiter the enemy position that lay ahead, before assaulting. Once on the top, I could not see well through the trees that shielded the target. So I slowly got to my knees, pulled out my binoculars, and started peering through them to get a better picture of what lay ahead.

That was when I met my "military death." Another lieutenant who was serving as a referee, a Lt. Donaldson, tapped me on the helmet and said, "You are dead. A sniper just shot you between your eyes when you got up on your knees.

That was devastating to me, because I took so much pride in being a platoon leader, and besides that, the commanding general and regimental commander were on the other hill viewing the simulated attack. I immediately ordered my platoon sergeant to take command and lead the attack, which he did successfully.

I returned to company headquarters and reported to our company commander, Captain Jim Lear. He told me he had already heard. I held my helmet in my lap and sat dejectedly before his desk. His advice to me was, "Shake it off and go back to your command." That I did, and apparently I was able to "get back on my horse and ride again," because soon after he made me company executive officer in addition to my position as platoon leader. That's when, in his absence while on a leave, I led our company in such successful maneuvers that we received regimental awards for the best company in the regiment. And I was promoted to first lieutenant.

After our 10th Division was flown to Fort Bragg, North Carolina, to take part in the first simulated atomic blast maneuver, we were reassigned to Fort Riley, Kansas (home of former General George C. Custer). Our entire 10th Infantry Division (now known as the Mountain Division) convoyed from North Carolina to Kansas, camping in pastures along the way. I was assigned the head jeep to lead the convoy across the country.

One stop along the way was at Fort Campbell, Kentucky, home of the 101st Airborne. On the first morning of our few days there, a Lt. Larry Franck, my dear friend from Ole Miss who was a paratrooper, came into our area and said to one of the sergeants, "I know 20,000 troops are moving through here, but would you happen to know a Lt. Berman? The sergeant's reply was, "Yes, sir. He's standing right over there, by the fire."

What a coincidence. He took me to the Officer's Club where we listened to our favorite forties and fifties music and got to spend some quality time together before my 10th Infantry Division moved out and on our way to Fort Riley, Kansas. During our tenure at the University of Mississippi, Larry was editor of the *Daily Mississippian,* and I was vice president of the Associated Student Body (ASB). Together we actually drafted, wrote, and signed the ASB constitution for the University.

Back to that tactical "death" experience I talked about earlier. As embarrassing as it was to me at the time, it was probably the best lesson I could have ever learned in the military. Had my division ever been called to fight in Korea or anywhere else, I can guarantee I would have never raised my head that high; and I would always have kept it down when peering through my binoculars to reconnoiter an enemy position!

Our "George" company—or "G" company for short—had a first sergeant named Delgado. He was a strapping man, six feet, three inches tall and 300 pounds. If he had been given the opportunity, he probably could have played on any NFL team in the country. He was a strong warrior, but also a kind individual. He had a great heritage: one parent was Hispanic and the other was African American. If I had ever been called to lead our company or my platoon into battle, this is the one person I would have unequivocally wanted to have by my side.

Just prior to my retirement from the military and departure for home, Sergeant Delgado came up to me and presented a beautiful handcrafted marble pen set for my desk, as a gift from the company to me for my leadership and dedication to the service. It was engraved as follows:

Lt. Robert Berman

April – 1955

Even today, that pen set sits proudly on my desk. I will always cherish that gift as a reminder of the time I served my country with some of the finest men and Americans I have ever had the good fortune to know.

8

My Summer in Europe— With Girls Galore

I completed my tour of duty with the 10th Infantry Division in the spring of 1955. After departing Fort Riley, Kansas, where I was last stationed, for my home in Lexington, Mississippi, I planned to continue my education for an advanced degree in business—an MBA. I applied to three of the best MBA programs at that time—the Harvard Business School, the Columbia Business School, and the Wharton Business School at the University of Pennsylvania, but my first choice for an MBA was the Harvard Business School. I was promptly accepted at Harvard and Columbia, and immediately agreed to matriculate to Harvard that fall. That decision was most fortuitous, as it set in motion events that determined the remainder of my life.

Prior to entering Harvard, my grandfather Morris Lewis Sr., who had always been so generous, offered my sister, Joan, and me each $5,000, which we could use to take a trip to Europe for the summer or use for something else. I chose the trip to Europe for six weeks. While over there I joined a tour that had five guys and eighteen girls, which made it a very interesting and enjoyable summer. Since the tour did not begin until a week after I arrived in London, I decided to explore the countryside alone before joining it.

Upon arriving, I checked into a small quaint London hotel. This was 1955, only a few years after the end of World War II, and many of the buildings in London were still bombed out shells from the Nazi blitzkrieg that had literally almost demolished the entire city. After checking in, a lovely French maid knocked on my door and offered to press my clothes. She was dressed in a black-and-white lace outfit, with a very short skirt; she was attractive enough for me to take a "second look." However, I was wise enough to only accept her offer of a pressing, as my clothes were somewhat wrinkled from the long flight over.

Evening was just starting to set in. I could see the lights of London begin to twinkle out my open window (no air conditioning in those days). There was something else that caught my attention. A melodious voice came through my window, singing with a band accompaniment. I'll never forget the sweet sound of her voice as she crooned "Volare." So I followed the sound down to the small lobby, out the door, and down the steps of a bombed-out church next door. In the cellar of that former church was a bar, and the source of that melody. Her voice was like that of a nightingale, and so soothing that I spent the next couple of hours just sipping a French wine and listening to my heart's content.

The next day, I decided to visit a good friend of mine from Ole Miss who was stationed at a U.S. Air Force SAC base in the northern part of England. I caught a train from London Station and headed for my rendezvous with Lt. Abe Tahir.

I had never ridden on a train where each compartment was enclosed with no way to enter the next compartment. On the way up to Abe's base, there was only one other person in my compartment—a young, well-dressed woman in her midtwenties. She was a schoolteacher, and the thought came to me that she might be somewhat uncomfortable since I was the only other person in that compartment and of the opposite sex. I was properly dressed and occasionally chatted with her in a friendly and pleasant manner, which I believe eased her mind. I spent most of the time gazing out at the colorful English countryside with its rolling hills and at the many sheep that grazed on them, similar to cattle back home in the United States.

When I arrived at the Air Force base, Abe met me and showed me around, explaining that General Curtis LeMay, who commanded the Strategic Air Command (SAC), had planes flying continuously night and day around the globe, to be certain our country was prepared to strike on a moment's notice. (This was before our long-range rockets were all in place and in subs around the world.) After a couple of days with Abe, dining in his officer's mess, he had his WAC secretary take me back to the train station, where I again boarded a train going still farther north, to Scotland. Once it arrived in Edinburgh, I checked into a hotel and decided to walk the famous Royal Mile between two significant locations in the history of Scotland, namely Edinburgh Castle and Holyrood Palace. It is the busiest tourist street in the Old Town.

Later that day, I inquired with the concierge about social activities for the evening. He happened to mention that there was a public dance hall open that night and gave me directions. After taking a cab—it was too far to walk—I arrived and entered a large gymnasium-style dance hall crowded with adult dancers of all ages and sizes. When I went over to the concession stand to purchase a coke, there standing next to me was a lovely blonde young woman of about eighteen to twenty years of age. Her blue eyes literally sparkled, enhancing her ruby red lips, which resembled those of Angelina Jolie's today.

We began a conversation. She seemed somewhat taken by my Southern accent, which was about as foreign to her as my Mississippi home. I learned she was a ballerina and part of the ballet company of Edinburgh. That was unexpected as she was so "well endowed," unlike most ballerinas who are not nearly as buxom. I asked her to dance, and she was a willing partner. There was an odd way the dance floor participants moved, always dancing in a circular motion. We danced the night away, very closely, and I did not want to stop. Then the lights began to flicker, letting all the dancers know it was time to close for the evening.

She asked if I would take her home, and I naturally consented. As we walked out of the dance hall, I spotted a large black cab and signaled the driver to pull over. Just before we drove off, I noticed she ducked her head down below the driver's seat. Thinking she might be ill, I asked her what was the problem. She replied, "That was my boyfriend who just crossed the street in front of us, looking for me, and he has a terrible temper." Had I known that in advance, I probably would have ducked myself, but the cab drove off as she moved closer.

She lived quite away from the center of the city, out in the countryside. That made the round-trip cab fare rather steep. However, it was worth the trip: we were alone in the darkness of the spacious backseat until we approached her home. At that point she asked me to stop the cab and let her out. I asked why not stop at her home, because it was late and dark outside. For whatever reason, she said she preferred to walk the last block alone. I waited until she turned toward one of the homes about a football field away, and then the cab drove off. We never saw each other again. That was quite an interesting evening.

I took an early morning train back to London and checked into the hotel where our tour was to begin. Sharply at 9:00 A.M. the next morning, we met with the tour guide in a private section off the lobby. He was a young man of average height and weight, dressed in a blue blazer sport coat and tie, who spoke with a New England accent. His name was Don, and I will never forget that first briefing. Most of the eighteen girls on the tour were quite pretty, fashionably dressed, and in their late teens or early twenties. As a matter of fact, I could have closed my eyes and imagined that I was back at my alma mater, Ole

Miss, with its beautiful coeds and later, the home of three Miss Americas. Over the next six weeks, I enjoyed the opportunity to share experiences and develop friendships with a number of them. One very attractive young lady in the group (one of the prettiest I had ever seen) and I became especially close. However, none of these companionships ever continued after the trip, and it was best that they didn't: as a year later, in Boston, I met the one woman I wanted to be my partner for the rest of our lives.

We sailed home on the Queen Mary, which is now docked as a historical tourist attraction in Long Beach, California. Upon docking in New York and shortly after arriving home, I matriculated to Harvard's Business School (HBS) and began an entirely new way of learning. It was, and still is, known as the Case Study method—HBS's premier decision-making and leadership curriculum.

Part II

Building a Future

9

Harvard Business School— And Finding My One True Love

When I began classes, I had to learn how to use a slide rule to calculate the many marketing, financial, and production cases we had. There were no computers or even calculators at that time.

I performed miserably on my first two examinations. I had been a first lieutenant and platoon leader in the U.S. Infantry for the past two years, and I was used to giving orders and expecting them to be obeyed without question. One of my first exams was a case study in human relations. My only inclination was to give orders and expect them to be carried out. I should have paid more attention to what was written and shown better listening skills, before making my conclusions and decision as to what needed to be done. I quickly learned from that first experience and the second one too.

The second exam was a case study in marketing. One of my HBS marketing professors happened to be Jim Parks, a former marketing professor at the University of Mississippi, with whom I had studied. He had written a book about marketing. I went to him the night before and asked if I could borrow the book he wrote to review it before the case study exam. He said, "Sure, but it won't do you any good." I took it anyway, and spent several hours that evening reviewing it. He was right. One of the first things you learn at the Harvard Business School is that studying and memorizing will do you no good. Instead, the real key to solving a case-study exam was using your ability to quickly read the case, summarize it, determine if there was a problem and if so, what it was and what needed to be done to rectify it. In other words, just use your brain.

Another challenge for me was to learn to read blueprints in 3D. Until then, I had never even looked at a contractor's set of blueprints. After many hours of concentration, I managed to master that, too. It took me a short while to catch on to all the new challenges and ways of thinking presented to me by the business school, but once I did, I graduated in the upper half of my class two years later.

MY ONE AND ONLY TRUE LOVE

One Sunday in Boston, during my second year at Harvard, I was invited to dinner at the home of a distant family member and his wife. He was a dentist and had also invited a young married couple. The husband of that couple asked me if I would like to meet someone with beautiful eyes and a voice to match. I responded, "Why not? Of course."

That simple question led me to call the person in question. We met a week later. She was, and still is, radiantly beautiful. I noticed her big, sparkling brown eyes, dark brown (almost black) hair, a sultry look, and a personality that could attract anyone. She was in her senior year at Lesley College in Cambridge, located across from the Harvard Law School, and studying at the New England Conservatory of Music. It was later that I also discovered her magnificent voice, with which she could have sung at Carnegie Hall or starred as the lead in Carmen—had

I not taken her as my bride six months later, after which we moved to Mississippi to begin our life together. My only regret is that I took her away from what could have been a highly promising musical career. I am thankful she does not have the same regret.

From the very first time I laid eyes on her, I knew she was more than special, she was someone I had been looking for all of my life, and here she finally was. I knew I would never let her go, once I found her.

Two months later my parents, Fay and Joe, and my young sister, Brenda (born eighteen years after me), traveled to Boston to meet her. We had dinner at a famous Boston restaurant known as Locke-Ober's, where only men could dine on the first floor. Thus we were seated upstairs. Afterward we attended a theater performance. During dinner, while I briefly left the table, my precocious six-year-old sister turned to Sondy and intuitively asked her a rhetorical question, "I know my brother likes you, but, how do you feel about him?" While surprised, Sondy was not flustered and obviously gave the answer that those at the table hoped to hear, as they all could not have been more impressed with her (even though they had not even heard her magnificent singing voice at that time).

Her answer was doubly confirmed a few weeks later when I received a call from her one evening. She told me she had just returned to her dormitory early from a date, and there was still time to see me before curfew. Her date had been someone else she knew who had recently returned from an army tour overseas. However, she had apparently made up her mind that I was the one she truly wanted to be with. That was the signal for me. I knew it was time for me to capture her heart and make her my soul mate for the rest of our lives. I was determined to not let that opportunity, or her, slip away! I hurriedly opened my drawer and took out my diamond Phi Ep fraternity pin to give her as my pre-engagement gift. When I arrived she was waiting for me on the porch of her dormitory. Once she saw me, she ran down the steps and into my open arms. We immediately got into my car and drove to a secluded place on the banks of the Charles River (that separated her college from the HBS). When I proposed to her and she promptly accepted, I reached in my pocket to give her my pin, and lo and behold, it was missing. I assumed I must have dropped it in my haste to see her. Instead, I gave her my gold ring with my initial "B" on it, which my parents had given me after my graduation from Ole Miss. We drove back to my parking lot and looked for the pin but to no avail. That really didn't matter to me because what I sealed that night was the most important thing I'd done in my life—then, and ever since.

Sondy has been my love, my inspiration, my confident, my best friend, my advisor, and my helper—without whom I could never have done the things I did—throughout our entire life together.

Incidentally—and amazingly—someone found that fraternity pin somehow realized it was mine, and gave it to me the next day, after I had related the incident to some others in the dormitory.

I must say I am thankful that Sondy and I met during my last semester at "B-School" (business school), as it would have been almost impossible for me to have courted her as I did before that time, due to the heavy workload and case studies we were expected to carry.

One of my favorite stories I tell is about one of Sondy's first experiences after we moved to and settled in the town of Indianola, in the heart of the Mississippi Delta region. It goes like this . . .

We first rented and occupied a small, yellow, two-bedroom house, across from the high school on one side and a sprawling cotton field on the other. The first morning after I had left for work, there she was, standing at the screened door, staring out at nothing but row after row of cotton plants. Since she had just moved from the active and busy New England environment and city of New Haven, Connecticut, home of Yale University, where she grew up, she understandably raised her outstretched arms, looked upward, and cried out, "Lord, O Lord, help me!" And the word came down . . .

"I would help you, but—where are you!?"

Actually, she promptly acclimated and became a "Southern Belle" overnight!

10

GRADUATION, MY FIRST JOB, AND A LOT MORE

Sondy and I were married on August 18, 1957, just six months after we had met. She had recently graduated cum laude from Lesley and I had my MBA from Harvard. But she was by far the best thing I ever got out of my two years at the Harvard Business School.

I had already begun work at my first job with a family regional chain of supermarkets, Sunflower Food Stores, headquartered out of the Mississippi Delta town of Indianola. It was run by two of my uncles, who offered me a salary that was considerably less than what my classmates were being offered elsewhere. It was actually less than what I was earning as a first lieutenant in the military two years prior to that. After some minor negotiations, they raised their offer slightly. Nevertheless, I took the job because I knew I could bring something of value into the family business. With my management skills, acquired from Harvard and the military, my goal was to take over the management of the firm and build the company to major proportions as I progressed through the ranks. A cousin of mine, Henry Paris, had graduated with a master's degree from Michigan

State University a year earlier. He told me that I was responsible for getting him a raise in the same company—he was receiving what they had initially offered me before they increased it—and they raised his salary to the same new amount. Sondy began teaching first grade at the local school, and later became the choral director at a nearby community college, to supplement our family income.

I moved from transportation management to sales manager to director of development of Sunflower Food Stores. Being director of development included everything from developing franchise stores to selecting locations, to negotiating leases, to financing the new stores and real estate where there was no outside investor. We were developing a new Sunflower Supermarket each month. Since we were expanding so quickly, I attempted to convince my uncles to take the best two or three sites each year and buy the real estate property, in addition to the stores located on the property. A successful supermarket chain in Texas, known as Weingartens, used that approach, eventually sold its supermarket chain, and successfully stayed in the real estate business. However, my uncles decided not to enter the real estate market as owners and instead put their funds into equipment and new stores.

After nine years at Sunflower, even after some significant salary increases—yet no clear sign of a path past my uncles (who were still relatively young) to the top of the company—I decided it was time to move on at the age of thirty-five. I had managed to acquire an option on a forty-acre tract of land at the confluence of two interstate highways, I-55 and I-20, in Jackson, Mississippi. I offered that option to my uncles at no profit, and they refused. Thus with an option and a prayer, I took Sondy, Marjie, and Debbie (two of our three daughters, with whom we had been blessed by that time) and moved to Jackson, Mississippi, our state's capitol.

After getting my real estate brokerage license and becoming a Realtor, I developed one regional and two neighborhood shopping centers, and later a multilevel office building with Prudential as the major tenant. Each property produced income for me for years to come.

MY DAYS AS A COLLEGE TEACHER

While I was studying for my real estate brokerage license, some staff member at Belhaven College in Jackson learned of my MBA from the Harvard Business School (HBS), and contacted me about the possibility of my teaching a class at the college, using the "case study" method introduced and utilized so successfully at HBS. Since I had the time and needed the extra income, I agreed to teach a semester night class there with that method. They gave me the option of selecting any subject I chose. Two of the most interesting subjects I studied at Harvard pertained to human-relations. I will never forget those two professors, one of whom had five marriages and who had, during the course of those marriages, learned a lot about life: what to do and what not to do to be successful. The other professor, George Lombard, a pioneer in the fields of human relations and organizational behavior, eventually became senior associate dean of the Harvard Business School.

Because of their influence, I designed and taught a course in human relations because I felt learning to communicate, deal, and get along with other human beings was one of the most needed abilities in life. The school advertised my class as a new course using Harvard's case study method, and a large number of students signed up for it.

One of my students was a vibrant young Catholic nun named Sister Dorothea Sondgeroth. She was unquestionably the most active and intelligent student in the entire class. Frankly, I learned a lot more from her than she likely ever learned from me. It was a joyful experience for me to be able to teach her some of the skills that I had learned at HBS, especially in human relations. Later in her career, she became the highly successful director of St. Dominic Hospital in Jackson, one of Jackson's major hospitals and health organizations. She served on the boards of many major organizations and received a large number of awards during her tenure. She recently retired, but continues to work in their charitable and fund-raising division. She kindly credits some of her success to the human relations skills learned from me in her earlier career.

Another student, who worked for the Jackson *Clarion Ledger* approached me at the end of the course and after the final exam, and asked if I would raise his written exam grade from a C to a B-, which could affect his final grade. He said that would help improve his position with the daily newspaper.

While there may be a best approach, there usually is more than one way to solve a problem. Thus I reviewed his written analysis and determined that not only did he not solve the problem, he never even correctly identified it and only wrote on the periphery. As compassionate as I try to be, under those circumstances, in all good conscience I could not accommodate him. It would have been against my principles and unfair to the other students in the class. It was also too late to allow him to write a paper for extra credit. He may remember my refusal; I recall being fair.

PART III

LIFE-CHANGING TRAGEDY

11

A Tragedy That Changed My Life

While I was teaching at Belhaven College, a tragic accident occurred in our family that changed my future business career. My dear father, Joseph E. Berman, a retired full colonel in the U.S. Army, an attorney, and a food broker, met a tragic and early death at sixty-seven years of age in a commercial airliner crash. A private plane ran into the commercial airliner he was on three minutes after takeoff in Hendersonville, North Carolina. All eighty-one passengers on the plane were killed. My father had been on his way to the famous Greenbrier resort in West Virginia to accept a trophy as the country's best food broker representing Stokely-Van Camp, a national canned-goods company of fruits and vegetables.

When I was a child, we lived in Atlanta, Georgia, where I was born. My father was a successful young attorney there. Moreover, he was a vital part of the community. As a member of the Jewish faith, he took on the Stone Mountain ultraconservatives and defeated their Ku Klux Klan candidate for a seat on the Atlanta city council. As a member of that council, my father was chairman of the airport committee and was responsible for bringing aviation to that growing city. He received this letter of commendation from Clark Howell, editor and general manager of *The Atlanta Constitution,* dated November 3, 1931:

Hon. Joseph E. Berman
Attorney-at-law
Atlanta

Dear Joe:

Thanks for yours of the 30th ultimo [last month] with enclosure of booklet of ordinances governing aviation in Atlanta.

I will, between now and next Sunday, take up the matter along the line of your suggestion, handling the subject not only in a local article, but with editorial comment.

I do not know what Atlanta would have done without you as chairman of the aviation committee of council. You have rendered the city splendid service in the development of its aviation field and have done more for it than has been done by another man or set of men.

Some of these days you should have a monument there, testifying to the excellent service you have rendered.

Sincerely, your friend,

Clark Howell
Editor
The Atlanta Constitution

A plaque with my father's name on it adorned the main gate to the Atlanta airport until Delta's expansion of the property. It now rests in the Atlanta archives. His law partner, former Atlanta mayor Alfred Sims, had been encouraging him to make a run for mayor of Atlanta when fate intervened.

Before my father's death in the airline accident, when we were living in Atlanta, my mother's mother, Julia Lewis, was killed in an automobile accident coming from Memphis to her home in Lexington, Mississippi. Her brothers Morris and Celian wanted my mother, Fay, to move back to Lexington to take care of her father, Morris Lewis Sr., who was severely injured in that same accident. She agreed, and my father gave up his successful law practice, promising political career, and a seat on the Atlanta City Council for the woman he loved, and moved to the rural Mississippi town of Lexington, population 2,500 at that time. Since there was little business for an attorney in that small town, he did the natural thing by beginning a food brokerage business to sell to my grandfather's wholesale grocery company and any others my father hoped to develop (which, in fact never happened except to a minor degree)

My father treated all of his customers equally when it came to prices, deals, and services offered. He was one of the most trustworthy human beings who ever lived. Despite that, it was extremely difficult for him to develop a significant business with customers other than the Lewis Grocer Company and the Sunflower Food Store chain, since he was the brother-in-law of Morris and Celian Lewis. Because possible potential customers were not acquainted with my father personally, they questioned whether they could receive the same good deals from my father's company that were offered to the company owned by his brothers-in-law. Unequivocally they would have, but one can understand their reluctance and how they might feel they were indirectly doing business with the "competition." Under those circumstances, my father was put in an almost untenable position businesswise. He was able finally to accept the situation and was content to own and operate a small yet profitable food brokerage company.

Joe Berman loved life so much that he didn't worry about his thwarted business plans that were beyond his control. He had so many other humanitarian and religious interests, was a world traveler, and wrote a novel entitled *With Apologies to No One.* In 1966 he visited Israel, Jordan, Egypt, and Lebanon, even though it was dangerous for a member of the Jewish faith to visit Mideast countries (except for Israel). In one country, as he was leaving his hotel to depart for the airport, an Arab came up to him, with a knife in his hand, and asked "Just what is your religion?" My father, realizing the danger he was in and replied, "My religion is goodness." He was really speaking the truth. The baffled Arab walked away, and my father got into his car to be driven to the airport. Upon his return to America, he gave many lectures and color-slide presentations to churches, synagogues, and civic clubs about his trip to the Holy Land. Many attendees stated that because they would likely never have the opportunity to visit that part of the world, my father in effect brought the Holy Land to them.

One lady came up to him after he made a presentation at her church, introduced herself, and said, "Mr. Berman, I must say you are a true Christian." My dad responded, "Thank you, Mrs. Smith, for that high compliment, and I want you to know that you truly have a beautiful Jewish heart."

The close family ties between my two uncles and my father (he was their only brother-in-law), and the importance of their business to his brokerage company did later detrimentally affect me. While I respected both my uncles and their business acumen, I did not have the same close, personal relationship with either of them as did my father. Yet the marketplace still recognized this continued family relationship.

After taking over my father's business, subsequent to his fatal accident, I knew I had to grow the business if I was to be successful and satisfied. I needed to convince the entire market, both potential customers and the principals we presently represented (along with potential new ones), that I, as my father, would be just and entirely fair in all deals, promotions, and services offered to everyone involved. From a historical standpoint that wasn't an easy task, but by personally meeting with each individual potential customer and principal, I convinced them. With considerable diligence and tenacity I became accepted, and in time I made the company work to everyone's advantage—including all of my customers and those we represented.

12

HOW I ALMOST LOST
THE COMPANY

Before convincing my customers and principals that I would be a fair and equitable partner, I had another major business obstacle to overcome. Once I assumed the management and ownership of my father's food brokerage company following his tragic accident, I almost lost control of it.

The management of SuperValu, the company that eventually merged with and took control of my uncle's wholesale grocery company and chain of supermarkets, did not allow their new company to continue the close relationship with my father's former brokerage business. While there was never any favoritism by my father given to my uncles' company before his demise, under current conditions, the new controlling partners felt it best for that relationship to cease altogether so there could never be any question of favoritism given to SuperValu. They believed such an impression would indirectly and eventually be harmful to SuperValu, especially since it was a public company listed on the New York stock exchange, and my uncle, Morris Lewis Jr. ultimately became chairman of the board of SuperValu.

To my dismay, their decision directly affected me. Even though I was not a brother-in-law and thus one step removed from that relationship, they insisted that I cease my new management of the food brokerage company and give up my ownership since I was so closely related. Otherwise, they could cease doing business with me, which in effect would have been the "death knell" to my company since they were my primary customer. Irrespective of my real estate developments and other entrepreneurial endeavors, I intended to grow this sales and marketing company as it had the potential of becoming my primary source of income.

I flew with my attorney, Larry Franck, and my CPA, Fred Ray, to SuperValu's headquarters in Minneapolis to appeal to their sense of fairness—but to no avail. In the first ten minutes of a meeting with a high company official, I stated my case, which I felt was more than reasonable and should be accepted. This was especially so since my father had established that business and given up so much to even begin it, ending with his life lost in that airline crash on a business trip. Neither was I as closely related to the Lewis brothers as my father had been.

The SuperValu executive was completely unsympathetic and did not change his opinion that I must abandon my ownership and employment in my own company. His mind was made up before I took off on the plane from Jackson. Promptly after I made my appeal, he stood up and in a cold-blooded manner said, "This meeting is over" and walked out of his own office without saying good-bye, good luck, or anything else, leaving us stranded with one other member of his firm. I was reminded of the business maxim: "Never negotiate in your own office, because you can't walk out." That apparently didn't apply to him.

The three of us left without saying another word. On the way home, I flew on a different plane than my associates, and as they were boarding, I gave them a victory sign, letting them know that I did not intend to let it end this way. As Winston

Churchill always said, "Never give up, never, ever, ever, ever, ever give up!" I was determined to not let anyone take away what should have been rightfully mine.

"NUTS"

During World War II, when Hitler launched a surprise major counteroffensive in December 1944, the 101st Airborne, then in France, was rushed into action and seized key road junctions at the Belgian town of Bastogne, where the Americans were quickly surrounded by the enemy. On December 22, four German couriers arrived at the American lines under a flag of truce with a written demand for the Americans to surrender in two hours or face annihilation.

Brigadier General Anthony McAuliffe, acting division commander in the absence of Major General Maxwell Taylor, remarked, "Us, surrender? Aw, nuts," and then wondered aloud how he should reply. Twenty-nine-year-old Lieutenant Colonel Harry Kinnard suggested, "With what you just said: 'nuts'." McAuliffe scribbled a response: "To the German commander: Nuts! From the American commander." On the way back to the defense line, a U.S. officer explained to the puzzled Germans that "nuts" meant the same thing as "go to hell." As history shows, the Americans did hold their positions, and the German's were ultimately defeated in the largest single battle of the war.

In effect, "Nuts" was my unstated but determined answer to the management of SuperValu. The only reason I didn't express or send my written answer to their unreasonable and unforgettable demand was that my company needed SuperValu as one of our major customers. Therefore I just did what I had to do and took whatever legal action necessary to protect my leadership and rightful ownership of my company—with the new name I had given it: Southern Food Brokerage—and my actions that followed were unequivocally successful!

TACTICAL MOVE:
A NECESSARY LEGAL MANUEVER

This is where my wife, Sondy, through her ingenuity, recommended a plan of action that saved the company for our immediate family ownership. During our years of operation, we had represented Chicken of the Sea, a national canned tuna fish company. Sondy and I had earned and been on several trips with other food brokerage owners who also represented Chicken of the Sea. In fact, I still own a Chicken of the Sea T-shirt that says "110% of Quota." One of those food brokerage owners was a fine gentleman by the name of Malcolm "Mac" Taylor; Sondy and I became good friends of Mac and his wife. He had a large food brokerage firm in Houston, Texas. During a National Food Brokerage Convention in Las Vegas, Sondy recommended to me that I ask Mac to "stand in" for me as a temporary, yet legitimate, purchaser of our company. He would legally represent to the industry, our customers, and principals (those companies whom we represented) that he was the new owner. The stock would legally be transferred to him in his name for one dollar and other good and valuable consideration. All the while, his stock would be held until I could repurchase it for a negotiated amount, reclaim it, and have it transferred back to me as my own. To convince Mac and especially his partner (who was not in favor of the plan), I accepted the financial help of my mother, Fay Berman, to purchase a large bond to protect Mac and his company against any losses they might incur and sustain during his temporary ownership of my company.

In sealing the deal, I flew to Mac's Houston offices with my CPA, Fred Ray, and another corporate attorney, the famous defense attorney Al Binder, and an associate. There we consummated the deal!

A SURREPTITIOUS MASQUERADE

Shortly after sealing the deal with Mac, our new company (continuing with its name of Southern Food Brokerage), gave two large and separate cocktail parties and dinners for our two major customers: Sunflower Food Stores (my uncles' company, which had just merged with SuperValu), and Jitney Jungle Stores. We held the cocktail reception in our offices on the third floor of my building, and the dinner in the fine dining restaurant known as Nick's on the ground floor below (a tenant of mine). During the cocktail reception, Mac Taylor, Southern Food's new legal owner, stood proudly in the reception line with me as I introduced him to my uncles of Sunflower Food Stores and the owners of the Jitney Jungle chain of supermarkets. It worked—all thanks to my ingenious wife, Sondy! I was therefore able to continue the true leadership of the business, and eventually, after a considerable period of time and for a reasonable amount of money, to repurchase it and quietly take back the stock ownership in my own name. No one ever questioned the background of how it all came about, nor was there ever a need to do so.

TRUST

Malcolm "Mac" Taylor was a trusted friend who could have legally kept the stock and refused to later sell and transfer it back to me in my own name. It truly was his company after the transfer. Yet I put my complete trust in him as he legally controlled the company and I realistically worked for him. He could have taken advantage of me and dismissed me, but he didn't. Any profits were absorbed by me and my management team in the form of bonuses. He was one of the most generous, trustworthy, and magnanimous gentleman I had ever had the good fortune to know. He did this strictly out of friendship and compassion. He did reap financial gain years later when I bought back the stock. However, I could never fully repay him for his part in helping to save our company for its rightful owner.

SOUTHERN FOOD GROWS

By bringing in top-quality people and remunerating them well, I grew the company from four to eighty-two employees, and expanded it progressively for the next twenty-eight years—guiding it through four mergers (the last one being the only one where we were not the surviving corporation). There were so many obstacles and details I had to overcome during those different mergers that to relate them would make this book too long to keep the attention of most readers. Suffice it to say I was successful in each one, consummating a fair deal for all involved. I always believed in the philosophy of "leaving some money on the table" for the other party so they too would feel they made a good deal. Unless both parties to a negotiation feel they have received their fair share, I contend it is not a good deal for either, as it could result in financial disadvantage for one of the parties or merely "hard feelings." It's always best that both sides walk away reasonably satisfied.

Nevertheless, one incident during my first merger was so interesting and unbelievable that I must relate it here. Brokerage representation was assigned by principals on the basis of territories. Our territory representation was limited because there were only two major food companies in Mississippi to whom we could sell.

Therefore, I made the decision to expand and enter the large market of New Orleans. Since there were several large and strong food brokerage companies in the Louisiana market, I felt it best, in military terms, to enter that large market from "the flank."

There were two successful but medium-sized food brokerage companies to the west of New Orleans, in Lafayette, Louisiana. I negotiated with each of them and made the decision to merge (buy) the one that I considered offered us the best possibility of success with the products they represented and the people they employed. Later, when I believed it was time to make a business assault into the New Orleans market, I relocated our Lafayette, Louisiana, headquarters into that bustling city.

Subsequently, the former owner did not move on with the company, and asked if I would sell three company cars to him and his family at reasonable prices. I agreed to do so without hesitation. We worked out monthly installment prices with no interest charges, to be paid over a year's time. About midway through that year, the checks stopped coming through the mail. I called a few times, and his daughter told me on each occasion that they had mailed their check—yet those checks never arrived. Finally I called one more time in exasperation, and to my amazement, the daughter told me the following story: She said she put the check in the mail, and someone had stolen the mail box! Anyone that could make up a story like that I decided needed to keep those three cars without any further payment due us. End of story.

Incidentally, it was in Lafayette where I first tasted alligator. It was a bit chewy, but sweet when dipped in seafood sauce. The only part of the alligator worth eating is the part of the tail next to the body. Otherwise, one cannot chew or digest its coarseness.

All during the time I was building my food brokerage business, I continued growing my real estate business and other entrepreneurial projects, including building and owning a 36,000-square-foot three-story office building in Jackson, where Prudential Insurance Company of America was our major tenant. I convinced them to lease a sizable space in our building by allowing them to place their large blue Prudential sign on the front of our bright white building. That enhanced our entire building in a big way! Our offices were located on the third floor. A bank, BancorpSouth, Delta Airlines, and our Pasta Factory restaurant (more about that later) occupied the ground floor.

13

ENTERING MAJOR LEAGUE FOOD BROKERAGE: THE SUPER BOWL AND SUPER BROKER SHUFFLE— ALL VICTORIOUS!

In the mid-1980s, before any of our four mergers, our company, Southern Food Brokerage, was competing with a larger food brokerage company for representation of the big Nabisco account. As a matter of fact, the brash owner of this particular company had sent me a message that they would be interested in buying my company. I sent back a message that we were not for sale, but would be interested in buying them out.

We had been representing a small number of Nabisco products in the supermarkets. Our competitor had been representing the major line of Nabisco products in those same supermarkets. Because we had less representation and had fewer sales reps, they were the huge favorite to "take it all."

Realizing this, I felt we needed to come up with a unique plan to win big in the interview with Nabisco, and as a result to secure their entire line of products for representation. Both companies—mine and my competitor's—had one shot at securing it all. Now, about that time the 1985 Chicago Bears football team, coached by Mike Ditka, won the Super Bowl.

Following the victory, some of its players put together a video where they sang and enacted what they called the Super Bowl Shuffle rap. It was unique, seen by millions, and attracted national attention.

Following the Bears' popular lead, I planned our own Super Broker Shuffle. I hired a local songwriter to compose the tune, to which I wrote the rap lyrics. Then I hired a choreographer to choreograph our shuffle.

I arranged for a TV studio, complete with makeup artists and so forth, to tape our Super Broker Shuffle. At that studio, we built a large display of Nabisco products, including all those we presently represented and all those for which we were competing. We dressed our three lovely secretaries in cheerleader outfits, and they opened the video with a dance and rap routine that introduced our sales and marketing team, along with their performances. Each of our eighteen sales reps held a different Nabisco product in their hands and rapped the exciting and positive words I'd written about it. Before and after all the raps were completed, we all "supershuffled" to the words, "We are the best, the sales rep crew, bringing the Super Broker Shuffle to you; we're so bad, we know we're good, nobody messes with our neighborhood. We didn't come here looking for trouble, we came here to WIN the Super Broker Shuffle!" My rap was the last of the eighteen and began with the words, "I'm Bob Berman, and I'm mighty proud to be a member of this Super Crowd." We all wore T-shirts with the Southern Food Brokerage (SFB) logo, and ended our rap by shouting in unison the letters SFB! This Super Broker Shuffle can be found today on YouTube (http://youtu.be/TDItzDzHY2M).

We won that direly needed representation, not because of the Super Broker Shuffle, but because it was determined by Nabisco Management that we had the best and most exciting company to be their overall marketing representative in our large territory. Of course, the ingeniousness of the Super Broker Shuffle did demonstrate the originality and uniqueness we could bring to selling their products in our marketing area. It also always helped them—and the management of other companies as well—to remember who we were. This win catapulted our company into the big-time major league food brokerage business—and we never looked back.

JAY LENO—AND THE SUPER BROKER SHUFFLE

One of Jay Leno's *Tonight Show* writers apparently viewed our Super Broker Shuffle on YouTube and showed it to him. Out of all the smooth and cool raps given by our sales reps, two were comically and unintentionally offbeat, likely due to their nervousness during the final taping of the show. On one of Jay Leno's shows, he asked his audience if they would like to see one of the worst raps ever made. Then showed a clip of only those two offbeat raps. The clip received a big laugh from the *Tonight Show* audience and propelled us, though unnamed, even more into the history books.

STAYING ON THE CUTTING EDGE

As our company grew, we continued to explore cutting-edge innovations in the food brokerage business. We were one of the first in our marketing area to install a computerized retail shelf alignment program to assist our retail supermarket customers. By utilizing their own records of product movement, we were able to recommend the placement and number of facings (each particular product aligned on the shelves) of all grocery products on their shelves, including those we represented and those of our competition. Even though it may have given some of our competitors' products an advantage over ours, the assistance we gave our major customers and their respect for our company and its innovative technology more than compensated for that. Our major customers also had their own computerized programs, but combining theirs with ours gave them much better accuracy and control of their shelf management. All of this went a long way toward maintaining and growing our business.

SOUTHERN FOOD BROKERAGE'S FINAL MERGER

As time passed, I recognized that the retail sales and marketing food brokerage business was rapidly changing. National retail companies such as Walmart and others demanded to be serviced in all of their stores, nationwide, by the same sales and marketing food brokerage organizations instead of dealing with a number of separate companies in different areas of the country. This began a rapid trend toward consolidation and mergers of food brokerage companies into much larger organizations that could service the entire country and thus continue to represent their principals. Otherwise those major grocery principals would, by necessity, begin to form and utilize their own sales forces, even though more costly.

Our final merger was the only one where we were not the surviving corporation. It was with a larger company known as Sales Mark, with headquarters in Little Rock, Arkansas, and Bentonville, Arkansas (home of Walmart). Their primary markets were Little Rock, Memphis, and Bentonville. We were about one-third their size. They had what we needed— additional expansion of our territory, including access to their major customer, Walmart, and the opportunity for continued growth—and we had what they needed—an entrance to the big New Orleans market. We had previously established a strong position in the New Orleans market by respectively merging with two large food brokerage companies in that city, with the final merger taking control of one of New Orleans' largest, well-respected, and successful food brokerage companies, Backer-LeJeune. It was owned and operated by two highly capable business executives and fine southern gentlemen, Warren Backer and Clay LeJeune.

Final merger negotiations took place in Sales Mark's corporate offices in Little Rock. I met with their four owners and concluded what I believed to be a fair arrangement for both companies, and for myself. I took a position on the Sales Mark board of directors. Afterward I made a major study of the company, presenting it to the board with my recommendations for some important changes. At the board's requests, I made trips to Mexico exploring the possibility of opening a major sales operation in that country. During one of those trips "south of the border," the Mexican mafia blew up the lobby of the hotel at which I had reservations the next evening. Their mafia organization was far more dangerous than the "mob" I used to work for in my younger days as a musician.

I also found and helped establish and finance Sales Mark's move to a major central office in Memphis, Tennessee, and recommended and helped guide the company in a second merger in New Orleans with another major food broker with whom I had previously opened merger negotiations. This all continued to strengthen the company. After five years, I retired from Sales Mark.

I might add here that some former food broker friends of mine also merged their companies with other larger organizations, only to have those organizations eventually fail. I was fortunate that I chose to merge our company with an organization that had capable, trustworthy, and continued successful management.

Today, with additional mergers, that same organization, Sales Mark, is now known as Cross Mark, and is the second largest sales and marketing food brokerage company in America. They have a corporate campus in Dallas, Texas, home of their national office.

PART IV

OUR AMAZING
RESTAURANT
EXPERIENCES

14

GOING WAY BEYOND BAGELS WITH CHINESE CUISINE

How do a Jewish entrepreneur and his wife take their business skills way beyond bagels and introduce two new restaurant concepts to the metropolitan Jackson, Mississippi, market? Following are the fascinating and true stories about our adventures in both a Chinese and an Italian restaurant—adventures no one could ever have imagined unless they too experienced these amazing events.

BUILDING A RESTAURANT—FROM SCRATCH!

Once Sondy and I moved to Jackson and were blessed with our third daughter, Sheri, we noticed there were no Chinese restaurants in the city. One had tried doing business there but closed because their Chinese cooks would only cook the food, freeze it, and come in from another city on weekends to serve their customers. I can state, without equivocation, that no Chinese restaurant will ever succeed without full-time Chinese cooks.

I had read the famous Green Bay Packers' coach Vince Lombardi's book, *Run to Daylight,* where he always told his backs that whenever they saw daylight, run to and through it with all their might. I saw daylight—an opportunity in Jackson, Mississippi, to establish a successful Chinese restaurant. Sondy and I both enjoy Chinese cuisine, and after discussing the possibilities, we proceeded to open the first successful Chinese restaurant in Jackson, known as the Golden Dragon. My experience in the food brokerage business also tied together somewhat with the restaurant business.

Getting started wasn't easy. We first had to find a Chinese chef and manager. We found him in Greenville, Mississippi, managing a Chinese restaurant for an owner of two such restaurants in the city of Greenville (population 45,000 people). His name was Eddie. Proceeding from that point, we looked for a location and found one on North State Street, a major north-south artery of the city that used to be known as Highway 51 and ran through Jackson to Memphis and New Orleans. The facility we found was a closed Roy Rogers roast beef restaurant.

Since we did not have the full financial capability of starting a new restaurant venture, we sought investors from a small group of good friends who also were adventurous and had the financial resources to share in this investment venture. Among them was Harry Danciger of Memphis, Tennessee, who had his own company and was a representative of restaurant and hospital equipment. Harry was a fraternity brother of mine at Ole Miss in Oxford.

Other investors were Bill Pope, owner of a Trane Air Conditioner distributorship; a neighbor, retired Colonel George Smith, who fought the Japanese in the Pacific during WWII; Fred Ray, our CPA in my Southern Food Brokerage company, and now in our restaurant; and Bob Travis, an outstanding attorney in Jackson. That was a motley group who had no restaurant experience, except perhaps for Harry Danciger, who sold his equipment to restaurants. Experience, no. Opportunity, yes!

We took an option on the vacant restaurant building and began a search for Chinese cooks. That perhaps was the most difficult job with which to begin, as there was a dearth of Chinese families, especially cooks, in the Jackson metro area, which consisted mostly of Caucasians (65 percent) and African Americans (35 percent). There were a few Asians in the mix.

We advertised in various newspapers throughout the South and in some Northern cities as well. We also contacted a few Chinese restaurants in the larger Southern cities—Atlanta, Houston, Memphis, and such. Surprisingly enough, we received a flood of applications and calls.

Then came the time-consuming part of screening all the Chinese applications. A good number of them couldn't speak much English, so unless they demonstrated a great knowledge of the business, had long-term experience, and offered excellent references, we dismissed them from the beginning.

I even took my spare time from the national Food Brokerage convention in New York and stood in line at the Manhattan unemployment office attempting to find some potential Chinese cooks. It so happened that most every time I went to New York to attend that convention in December, I would catch a cold, or worse. My father-in-law, Stanley Shindell, offered a recommendation to cure that problem. He suggested that I shop for a heavy fur coat to keep me warm in that cold winter climate. I took his advice and found a heavy synthetic fur coat and Cossack hat, which definitely kept me warm and prevented me from contracting colds in extremely cold climates. Since the coat closely resembled a mink coat, many of the rough-looking men in the unemployment line eyed me so closely that I felt one of them might try to literally cut my throat to steal it from me. I was happy to leave the area as soon as I could, even empty-handed.

I also tried to find quality Chinese chefs when I went to Atlanta, assisted by my dear cousin Beryl Weiner. He took me to a number of top Chinese restaurants in that city, asking for their recommendations in locating Chinese chefs for our new restaurant in Jackson.

We finally secured the employment of four Chinese chefs who agreed to move to Jackson and work under the management of Eddie, our manager from Greenville, who had signed a management, noncompete agreement with us. One chef was from Shreveport, Louisiana, one was from Memphis, one was from Meridian, Mississippi, and one was from Houston, Texas.

Now came the even more important effort of settling these new chefs in the city of Jackson. Each one required that he be paid in cash for his work. Furthermore, we had to lease a home for them in which they could reside, as well as beds, bedding, cooking and eating utensils, towels, soap, and everything else that makes up a home. Actually, they did not need cooking and eating utensils, because they ate all of their meals at the restaurant "on the house."

After the chefs were hired, it was time to hire waitresses, kitchen helpers, and a bartender. We also had to locate a supplier of Chinese vegetables, fruits, and other ingredients that normally go with Chinese cuisine. Additionally, we had to restock the kitchen with woks, ovens, dishwashers, knives, spoons, forks, and all other types of kitchen equipment, and do the same for the customers as well—dishes, bowls, cups, saucers, and the stainless-steel serving dishes in which Chinese food was traditionally served. We were fortunate to have Harry Danciger as one of our investors; because he was in the restaurant equipment business, he knew exactly what we needed, and he helped us find a good amount of used kitchen equipment, tables, booths, and other such items.

All of this took an exceedingly large amount of time. I had my Southern Food Brokerage business to manage and could only take a certain amount of time away from it, so my wife, Sondy, stepped in and took control of the Chinese cooks and all of their multiple home needs. Harry Danciger handled the equipment and furnishing needs. I handled the lease and whatever financing we needed, and, along with Sondy and Harry, redecorating the interior.

After our equipment and furnishings were in place it was then time to bring in our manager, Eddie, put him on the payroll, and begin training the entire staff. We gave Eddie three weeks to get everyone trained and in shape for our opening, because until we opened, all of our cash reserves were going out but nothing was coming in. If we waited much longer to open, it would have depleted most of our cash reserves. After two weeks Eddie said he needed another two weeks to prepare. We gave him that and planned the opening, including advertising (which was a big mistake).

The week before the planned opening, Eddie came to us and said he needed more time to prepare. I personally refused that request. He had had plenty of time to train and prepare the staff. We needed to start the cash inflow and could not wait any longer. He understood and reluctantly agreed.

THE INCREDIBLE VANISHING EGG ROLLS

The week before our public opening, we served dinner to our investors. All went smoothly, and the food was absolutely delicious. I even had shark fin soup for the first time. Two days before our public grand opening, I had what I thought was a brilliant and prescient thought. I felt if anyone came into a Chinese restaurant and could not order an egg roll because the kitchen was out of them, it would be like trying to order a hamburger at McDonald's and being told they were out of them. What a faux pas that would be!

So I called my good friend Harry Danciger in Memphis. I asked him to go to a Chinese restaurant in Memphis (there were two), and buy 500 egg rolls and fly them to Jackson on the day before the opening so we would have enough and not run out. His reply was, "Make your own." I explained that is exactly what we did, but if we had a large crowd, the odds were that we would run out of them and that would not be well accepted by our new clientele.

Harry was a very close friend and terrific guy, but he was also one of the most prudent individuals I had ever met as far as money was concerned. To say he was frugal would be a major understatement. Finally he agreed to purchase those extra egg rolls and bring them to Jackson. However, the day before our opening, he was scheduled to fly to north Tennessee on a business call (he owned his twin-engine private plane). He agreed to purchase those egg rolls and fly them in the night before our opening, after his meeting.

That evening, he called me about 8:00 P.M. and said he was meeting his wife and kids at the airport for a quick dinner. They had picked up the egg rolls. Then he would fly them to Jackson. He planned to land about midnight at the Jackson International airport, where I was to pick him and the egg rolls up and take them to our restaurant.

At midnight, I was at the airport anxiously awaiting Harry and the 500 egg rolls. He arrived exactly on time and unloaded two large crates of egg rolls. I carefully helped him take them to my new station wagon. As we were loading the back of my station wagon, Harry said, "I flew at 10,000 feet to keep the egg rolls fresh, as they were not on ice." He reiterated to me that he had been on a sales call in north Tennessee that day, and flew in just in time to have dinner with his wife and two kids at the airport before taking off for Jackson. His kids had a cough and yet stayed up to see their daddy and have dinner with him.

While loading the egg rolls, I showed Harry the disappearing tailgate on my new station wagon. It did not open and shut—outward and upward—as on most station wagons and today's SUVs; rather, it went up and down and disappeared under the carriage at the signal from the remote I held in my hand. Harry said, "That's really neat. I'm going to try to have that unique feature on the next station wagon I buy for my family.

We both got into the car and promptly headed for the restaurant. On the way from the airport, he related to me that he only bought 300 egg rolls, not the 500 I had requested. When I inquired why, he said they were expensive, as the restaurant charged him full price, even though they did not need to cook or serve them. That upset him, so he only bought 300, which he felt was enough anyway. That was Harry's way of demonstrating his frugality, regardless of its consequences.

All the way to the restaurant, which was about ten miles away, Harry kept saying how he couldn't believe we were charged full price for the 300 egg rolls. I finally told him to forget it. Then along the way he kept asking me if I heard a sound like rushing air from some window that was open. I didn't notice anything unusual, so we continued to our destination. It was then about 12:30 A.M.

When we finally arrived, we blew the horn and our head chef and manager, Eddie, and Bill Pope (one of our investors) came out to greet us. As we went to the back of the station wagon to retrieve the two containers of 150 egg rolls each, to our utter amazement and astonishment there were no egg rolls in sight. We couldn't believe it, but quickly noticed that the disappearing tailgate had been left open after we departed the airport, and the egg rolls that had been so diligently planned for, purchased, and cared for, were "short coupled and long done"! None of us could believe the error I apparently had made in not using my remote to close the tailgate before we left the airport. Everyone felt awful, and I felt even worse in making such an uncalled-for mistake.

Immediately we jumped in the car and began to retrace our route in the pitch-black dark, with no moonlight to guide us, only our car headlights. All of our efforts were in vain, with the sole exception of when we turned back—about two blocks away from the restaurant—to drive up what I have ever since called "Egg Roll Hill." It appeared that in my anxiousness to get to our restaurant and unload our "precious cargo," I must have taken that incline and turn at a rapid rate of speed, especially at that time of the morning when little if any traffic was on the streets. That's when one crate of egg rolls slid out the back of the station wagon. We spotted it in the middle of the main street. We pulled over to the side of the road, jumped out, and to our dismay found only a crushed crate, scattered all over the street. The only things we found in one piece were a few egg rolls in the middle of the street. I picked up a few, put them in the car, and returned to the restaurant. Once there I showed them to our head chef who remarked, "They weren't good egg rolls in the first place. They were flat." I said, "If you had been thrown out of a car going about thirty miles an hour around a curve, and then been run over by a truck, you would be flat too." I was too old to cry, but too sad to laugh.

After Harry called his wife, Barbara, in Memphis at 2:00 A.M. and told her the unbelievable "Vanishing Egg Roll" story, she couldn't believe it anymore than we could, especially since she had taken her sick kids with coughs to pick up the order earlier the night before, then met Harry at the airport for a late dinner, and bade him a good-luck farewell for the opening the next day. After all was said and done, I told Harry, "I wish it had been your luggage, instead of the egg rolls that shot out of the back of the station wagon," but no such luck! Our investors thought about presenting me with an Egg Roll trophy, but decided it was too sad an event to recall in memory.

THE GRAND OPENING LUNCH

After I awakened my wife, Sondy, to tell her the absurd story of the "Vanishing Egg Rolls," which she was aghast to learn, we tried to get a few hours sleep in what remained of the night before arising early that same morning and driving to the Golden Dragon to help prepare for whatever guest patrons would arrive for lunch. When we arrived the chefs were naturally busy making additional egg rolls to hold in reserve when and if needed for our opening—and they were definitely needed. We almost ran out at lunch, and we still had a "Grand Opening Dinner" that night.

While we had trained our staff well and felt we were reasonably prepared for the grand opening, we made a crucial mistake prior to it. We were so excited about being the only Chinese restaurant in Jackson, which had been eagerly awaited by a large clientele who looked forward to dining on Chinese cuisine, that we, through a lack of experience, heavily advertised our grand opening date through the *Clarion-Ledger/Jackson Daily News,* the state's largest daily newspaper, and on several local radio stations. That did it! We had an overflow of customers for both lunch and dinner, especially at dinner.

Of course, most restaurants have "bugs" to work out at their initial openings. The first one I can recall was at lunch. One of our investors, an esteemed attorney, Bob Travis, brought several of his partners and some staff for lunch. They had a long table of about twenty patrons. I happened to be in the front of the restaurant when I noticed that one of our best waitresses, Diane, had been assigned to that table.

She was holding a large tray of water-filled glasses and beer. I noticed that it began to tilt, and the glasses started sliding like dominoes. Beer and water spilled all over Bob's table and on the coats, ties, and pants of several of the attorneys at that table. Our staff all quickly convened to clean up the mess and offered towels to the many who had been inundated with beer foam and water. Thank goodness these people were associates of one of our investors and that it was not another law firm that could have sued us for damages to fine suit attire that might have been permanently stained.

Somehow we managed to get through lunch without any other calamities, and then we began to prepare for the dinner hour.

THE GRAND OPENING DINNER

Our dinner hours began at 6:00 P.M., and nowhere in Jackson, a midsized city of approximately 400,000, had there ever been an opening as large as ours. Our restaurant comfortably seated 150 patrons, yet there were several hundred lined up all the way across the street, awaiting their turn to enter, be seated, and served. We had no idea there was such a pent-up demand for what we were offering, and our advertising definitely brought them in!

Initially everything went relatively smoothly, even under such packed conditions. However, it was truly a hectic evening, to say the least.

At one critical point in the dinner opening, Sondy literally saved the night. She had been supervising the hostess and assisting when needed. All of a sudden the newly hired head waitress rushed over to Sondy and said, "This is too much pressure for me. I'm leaving." As she was about to walk out of the restaurant, Sondy noticed she was holding in her hand a number of orders she had taken. In her haste to abandon her duties, she had forgotten to turn them over to another waitress. Sondy quickly responded and asked for the tickets. When the waitress handed them over, Sondy asked, "Which tables do these orders cover?" To which the waitress replied, "You figure them out." Thankfully, Sondy, a normally cool-headed person, had noticed the large table that the waitress had been near, so she took the orders, sorted them out, approached that table, and calmly reconfirmed who ordered what on each ticket. What a remarkable achievement; most people would have thrown up their hands and also quit—but not Sondy. Without her levelheadedness and ability to handle a critical moment, our grand opening night would have nearly been a disaster.

And yes, we did run out of egg rolls.

Earlier that morning, however, realizing that we might run out and after the fiasco in the early hours of that same morning when we lost 300 egg rolls in reserve, I went to Kroger Supermarket and Sunflower Food Stores and purchased all the frozen egg rolls they had in their freezers. When our homemade egg roll supply later began to get low, I went into our kitchen and amid all the woks and other preparations and cooking that was taking place, I found a big pot, filled it with cooking oil, located a vacant burner on the stove, and began cooking the frozen egg rolls en masse as a substitute for the real ones. Since many of the Jackson clientele were not as familiar with the best-made egg rolls (prepared homemade from our kitchen and chefs), they did not complain when we served them the ones that came precooked except for deep frying to make them crispy and ready to serve. That action also helped save the first night's opening, but it was nothing compared to the heroics of Sondy and the calm manner in which she took control of what could have been a calamity.

The cash inflow that day was huge and direly needed after months of outflow and no inflow, and we survived the opening lunch and dinner without any major breakdowns.

THE AFTERMATH

After our inglorious yet overall successful grand opening, we managed to handle the coming days and weeks in a reasonably successful way, all the while gaining needed experience with our staff, our chef/manager, Eddie, and even our investors. Things began to settle down, and yet the crowds continued to flow in, just not to the extent as they had for the grand opening.

Now that we had settled in and had time to catch our breath, I conceived the idea of having a second grand opening. The July Fourth weekend was approaching. While many cookouts would be on tap that weekend, I felt it would be a smart approach also to have a week-long second grand opening, offering specials at some discounted prices to attract the crowds again and get them into a normal, routine dining experience at our Golden Dragon Restaurant.

In the meantime and fortuitously, a lovely and petite young lady of Chinese descent came into our restaurant and applied for a job. The manager referred her to me, and she came into our Southern Food Brokerage offices for an interview. I was immediately taken by her looks, her demeanor, her intelligence, and the fact that she had experience working as a hostess in a large Chinese restaurant in another metropolitan Southern city.

Her name was Juli, but after hiring her, we immediately and benevolently began renaming her as our "Dragon Lady," from one of the comic strips. She fit the bill to perfection. We dressed her in Chinese silk gowns, and she looked the part. The only thing we had to teach her was to ask our patrons, "Is everything all right?" instead of, "Is anything all right?" With all her experience as a hostess, I couldn't imagine how that expression slipped into her vocabulary, unless it was needed in one of her previous employments.

For our second grand opening, we felt we were in great shape, had successfully survived and gone through the testing grounds of the first grand opening, and were ready for our real major test. At that point, even though advertising was the wrong thing to do for our first grand opening, we felt confident enough to give it another try. Thus the ads, circulars, and radio advertisement began to flow again, a week in advance of the date.

Unfortunately, that day came about all too quickly. The morning before we opened for lunch that day, I happened to drive over to our restaurant to check in and make certain all was in good order for our next big show. To my utter amazement, I saw our manager/chef in his car parked in front of the restaurant, bent over his steering wheel, as if he had just collapsed. I immediately opened the door on the driver's side and tried to awaken him, but he was in something of a trance. Finally, when I was able to arouse him, he was still in a stupor, and in no shape to lead his staff for that second big weekend.

I dragged him out of his car, put him in mine, and took him to the home of my uncle, Dr. Max Berman, one of the last family doctors who even made house calls, with one of the best bedside manners ever (which today seldom exists). He examined Eddie and said it must have been something he took to put him in such an unresponsive state. I explained our dire situation and asked if there was anything he could do to revive Eddie. He said he could ask Eddie if he would allow him to give him a shot that would stimulate him and help revive him. Even in his stupor, Eddie agreed. He then had to sign a document approving the treatment. After that shot, Eddie quickly woke up and momentarily regained his senses and composure. I decided to take him home and let him rest for the day, believing that our current staff of Chinese cooks could handle lunch. I took him to his home, put him to bed, and even removed his socks. He seemed to go into a deep sleep; the shot he received only temporarily revived him. It was later determined that he must have taken some drug, either prescription or otherwise, that put him into such a state. Anyway, with Juli (our Dragon Lady) at the helm and taking charge of the front end, and the several Chinese cooks we had hired for our kitchen and openings, we managed to once again successfully get through our second grand opening in reasonably good shape.

That's when I promptly dismissed Eddie and hired a new manager, albeit a Caucasian one. Nevertheless he had restaurant management experience and seemed quite intelligent, making a good appearance for our customers. We also had an abundance of Chinese chefs at the time, as backups to Eddie, and thankfully most of them spoke English and stayed with us.

OUR NEW BAR AND LOUNGE EXPERIENCE

When we initially renovated the former Roy Rogers roast beef restaurant, we set aside a small area for a bar to serve alcoholic beverages. We were aware that ours was a family-style restaurant; when most patrons came for lunch or dinner in

Chinese restaurants, they normally did not order cocktails—if anything they had a beer or some wine. Unlike many Chinese restaurants today, we served steaming hot tea in a kettle, together with small, decorated teacups and saucers at every meal with no charge.

After going through two reasonably successful grand openings and some weeks after without any mishaps, and confident in our Dragon Lady hostess, ample Chinese chefs, and a new experienced manager, Sondy and I decided to take a brief respite and spend a weekend with our three daughters on the beautiful Mississippi Gulf Coast at what was then the outstanding Beachfront Hotel—known as the Broadwater Beach Hotel. After driving three hours down State Highway 49, we arrived and settled in for a well-earned, relaxing weekend. My Southern Food Brokerage company was well staffed and competently managed, especially with a new sales manager I had just hired by the name of Ken Paissant from New Orleans.

After dinner, as we were retiring, I decided to call the restaurant to check in. Juli, our Dragon Lady, said I had better call one of our investors, our attorney Bob Travis. When I asked why, she informed me that our new manager and our head waitress and our bartender had all been arrested and were being held in jail. I was flabbergasted, and immediately called Bob Travis at his home. He informed me that earlier that evening, a young couple came into our bar, sat down, and ordered a gin and tonic and a vodka gimlet. Unfortunately our bartender did not ask to see their drivers' licenses to prove they were of legal drinking age (twenty-one in Mississippi). It so happened that they each were twenty years of age and looked every bit a couple who were legally of drinking age—but they were not. Shortly after they began to imbibe, two agents from the Drug and Alcohol Enforcement Agency came into the restaurant, checked their drivers' licenses, and arrested our bartender, manager and head waitress for serving alcohol to underage individuals. That was quite obviously nothing more than a set up by what we believed to be owners of one or more competing restaurants (not Chinese) who had lost some of their regular business patrons to our restaurant.

Bob Travis assured me that all was under control and that he had bailed them all out, personally going to the jail and paying somewhere around $2,000 for their release. Although our employees were shaken by this experience, nothing more came of it, but what a way to start what was supposed to be a well-deserved and relaxing weekend.

THE VANISHING CHINESE CHEFS

Besides the vanishing egg rolls, we also had what we called "vanishing Chinese chefs." To reiterate, there is no way to run a successful Chinese restaurant without good quality Chinese chefs.

Since there was a dearth of Chinese residents in Jackson at that time, there was no real way for our Chinese chefs to have any kind of meaningful communications and social life, except among themselves, and most of their time was spent cooking and sleeping. Therefore, it was understandable that from time to time some of our chefs would vanish in the night, and the next day we were left shorthanded in the kitchen until I could replace them. Luckily for us, they must have had a communication system among their fellow chefs, for no sooner had we discovered that a chef had disappeared than we would receive calls saying they understood we needed a Chinese chef—and they were available on short notice. That all worked well except for one particular incident. All of a sudden on a Thursday, we only had two chefs in the kitchen that morning; the others had vanished into the darkness of the night. I knew if we lost even one of them we would be in big trouble and not able to handle what had developed into a good and consistent clientele.

That evening, about midnight, after the last patron had departed, I went into our kitchen. The best of the two remaining chefs was named Bob Moy. I called him over, and we sat on large bags of rice and began to talk. I said, "Bob, if either one of you leave, we would be down to our last Chinese chef, and that would be an untenable and unacceptable situation for our restaurant." While he spoke and understood English, he pretended that he didn't. He looked intently at me and replied, "You no understand." I asked what he meant by that remark. He replied, "You're foreigner!" I guess, even in the great USA, to him I was the foreigner.

He then began to speak better English to me and said, "If you pay me double, I will do the work of two chefs, and you will not need to worry." I agreed to do so, as long as we were down to two chefs, and he truly did the work and put in the hours of two chefs.

That same day I had received a call from a Chinese chef in San Francisco. He spoke broken English, enough that I understood he was an experienced chef in a famous Chinese restaurant in that city's Chinatown. He wanted a change, for whatever reason, and he heard I needed another chef. As chancy as it may have been, I promptly purchased a one-way ticket for him from San Francisco to Jackson and sent it to him by Federal Express. He was to catch a "red-eye" flight and be in Jackson in time for the Saturday night rush-hour meal.

For whatever reason, and I can't explain it, in changing flights he somehow boarded the wrong connecting flight and landed in Greenville, Mississippi, ninety miles to the north of Jackson. I received a call from Greenville's airport security that a Chinese gentleman had arrived there by accident. He had given them my name and number to call. I told them to literally "chain him to the terminal lounge" and I would be on my way to pick him up. I immediately leased a private twin-engine plane (the only way I would fly privately, after some uncomfortable experiences in a single engine plane), hired the owner of the oldest and most reliable private airline company in the city, and had him fly me to Greenville to pick up our new misplaced

Chinese chef. We got him on board and promptly took off again for Jackson. We landed about 5:00 P.M. that Saturday afternoon and drove him immediately to the Golden Dragon, where we were greeted with cheers from our staff and waiting investors. He was quickly given an apron and a cleaver and began his new job as our third Chinese chef (actually four, since Bob Moy was doing the work of two chefs at the time, as we had agreed). Saved by the bell!

FRIENDS FOREVER?

Several months after we had opened, one evening I received a call about midnight, after Sondy and I had retired. It was one of our good friends. The husband said he and his wife had dined at our restaurant that evening, and he wanted to know if I was going to pay for her doctor's fees after they departed. I had no idea what he was talking about and asked him to explain. He said they had dined at the Golden Dragon earlier that evening, and his wife had become violently ill and had to be taken to the hospital. He explained that the emergency room doctor said it was from something she must have eaten. I stated how regretful I was about her illness, (which had subsided by then), but I would need to check into that matter the first thing the next day to see if anyone else had also become ill from dining there and consuming the same dish. He was persistent that I should pay her doctor and emergency room bill, but I continued to say I would check it out first thing the next day and get back to him.

That I did, and found out that no one else had complained of any illness from any food that evening, and several had eaten the same meal his wife had ordered. Furthermore, it was noted that she had been drinking heavily, ordering several drinks, which could have been the cause of her illness. Or it could have been a twenty-four-hour virus. I called my "friend" the next day, inquired about the health of his wife, and explained that I had checked and no one else had reported any illness from eating the same food as she had eaten. I stated that we were in no way responsible for her temporary sickness, and felt no obligation to reimburse any medical fees and expenses. He was not satisfied with my answer, and thus our friendship became a lot more distant. It was never pursued by them or brought up any further.

"WE ARE WATCHING YOU FROM ACROSS THE STREET"

One weekend, when the general manager went AWOL, I called my sister Brenda, who was born when I was eighteen years old and ready for college. She was a new radiologist in Birmingham, Alabama. I asked if she and her husband would come over and manage the restaurant for a long weekend, when she was off duty. I guess, as a young married couple without children, and having dined there before, they felt it was a good opportunity to pick up some extra dollars and eat as much fine Chinese food as they could enjoy. So they agreed to take my offer and quickly drove to Jackson on an early Friday morning. Once they checked in, all went fine, and I felt secure for the weekend and until our manager returned—that is, until midnight on Saturday evening, when I received a call from my sister's excited husband. He said, "We are being watched from across the street." I asked, "What are you talking about." He said, "We just received a call from someone who said they were watching us from across the street, and then they hung up." I knew we had taken in a large amount of money that weekend from several parties that dined there, and I needed to deposit the weekend funds in a nearby bank before closing. So I told my brother-in-law to go ahead and make the night deposit, and I would have a police escort for him. He told me in no uncertain terms, "I am not setting foot outside of this restaurant to make a night drop deposit, even if you have the National Guard to accompany me." So the funds were locked in our restaurant safe for the evening and the remainder of that weekend (which was dangerous too, had anyone realized it and robbed the establishment.) Nevertheless, my sister and brother-in-law got paid, had their fill of the best Chinese food around, returned to their home safely, and no one attempted to break into the business. "All's well that ends well."

THEN ALONG CAME JOHNNY LEE

Our current manager at that time became more unreliable and was not keeping regular hours. It was reported that most weekends he took a private plane to Texas, somewhere near the Mexican border. We never found out why, but it did seem strange, especially since his responsibility was to the Golden Dragon, and not to be absent on several weekends without notifying us of his intended absence or the reasons why.

Realizing we needed to change our management, we began a search for a more permanent manager on whom we could rely, someone who we could eventually make a partner or even sell our ownership to, if and when we were ready to move on to other ventures.

Having been in the food and commercial real estate development business most of my life, I had developed a plan and the intention of starting a chain of successful restaurants. However, we all quickly realized how difficult it would be to build a chain of Chinese restaurants, since one basic requirement was to have an abundance of reliable and quality Chinese chefs. That was almost impossible in communities the size of Jackson or other midsize cities, and the larger metropolitan areas already had mostly privately owned and a few chain-owned Chinese and Asian restaurants.

Bill Pope, one of our owners, reported to me that he knew of an excellent Chinese chef who was working for his uncle in one of Memphis, Tennessee's, two best Chinese restaurants. Harry Danciger, another owner (he of egg roll fame), also knew about this person, who was the head chef and assistant to his uncle in the exact same Chinese restaurant where he had purchased the now-infamous egg rolls the night before our opening. I was told the chef's name was Johnny Lee. Harry, who lived in Memphis, went to see Johnny at my behest and asked if he would be interested in becoming our general manager and head chef.

Johnny responded enthusiastically. He came to Jackson to be interviewed by our investment team. We were all impressed, especially since he was the chef that had made those 300 egg rolls that were lost on "Egg Roll Hill" the night before our grand opening. Besides that, he appeared confident, well skilled in managing people, and ready to take on the task as our new general manager and head chef. We hired him without further adieu. We wanted him to report to duty as soon as possible, before his uncle could persuade him to remain with him as his chief assistant. That he did, and we were really on our way to having a profitable venture for the next several years.

Incidentally, Johnny Lee Seto was unequivocally a full-blooded, purebred Chinese gentlemen. He was born in Canton, China—the Chinese had renamed Guangzhou after the Chinese communist regime took over. One day, during World War II, when Johnny was about six years old, he and his family were harvesting crops in a rice paddy when Japanese fighter planes, with bright red suns marked on their fuselage, swooped over and strafed all of those innocent civilian farmers. All ran for as much cover as they could find in the trees close by. In the turmoil and horror, many of the families who survived were separated. Johnny Lee was left alone in the rice paddy, terrified and screaming at the top of his lungs. Fortunately, one of the brave farmers saw him, ran into the open field, picked him up, and later reunited him with his family. Johnny never forgot that.

Later in life, Johnny's wife, Pauline, joined him from China, and even later so did his parents. Pauline came to work at the restaurant and was a good addition as a cashier and hostess. Johnny provided for all of them. He and Pauline had two children, Christine and Junior, who grew up in Jackson. Christine became a nurse, and Junior joined the fire department as a fireman.

BLOOD BROTHERS

In the early American West, cowboys and Indians became "blood brothers" by cutting their respective wrists and bleeding into each other's wounds. Johnny Lee and I did the same. One evening in the kitchen he was showing me how to handle the wok, and I accidently cut my wrist. Seeing that, he immediately took one of the sharpest knives in the kitchen and cut his own wrist. Then he put his wrist on top of mine, and we bled into one another before wrapping gauze around our wounds to stop the bleeding. From that time on, Johnny Lee and I were always "blood brothers"!

THE DRAGON BEGINS TO GROW

The first expansion of the Golden Dragon was at the front end of the restaurant. We added a larger main entrance where the patrons could enter from either side. We also added fancier ladies' and men's restrooms at the entrance area.

The second and by far the largest expansion came in the third year of our operation, when we had earned enough profit and continued cash flow to fund the next expansion.

Trader Vic's Polynesian Lounges and bars, featuring all kinds of Polynesian and regular cocktails, were in several larger cities and had made an impression on some members of our investment team. After considerable discussion and planning we decided to add a Polynesian lounge and bar to the front of our building, especially since there was ample room to expand toward State Street. There was no such lounge in Jackson, so we felt it would be a significant addition to our restaurant operation.

The lounge was extremely well designed. The tables and chairs were red and black bamboo and of Polynesian design, with large cushions; and they could swivel to either side. The bar had a thatched-roof overhang, and the wallpaper was white with a red bamboo design. There was Asian décor throughout. Bamboo lanterns hung from the ceiling, giving the room a calming and relaxing effect.

Before opening, Bill Pope and I sat at the bar half the night, sampling and naming various Polynesian alcoholic drinks—Mai Tais, Fog Cutters, and many others, mostly rum based. Once we had completed our task, we were fortunate to both arrive home safely. That's because we only sipped, not guzzled, while taste testing.

The lounge was designed with an upper deck, connected by a spiral staircase to the main floor. It was for private dining. One evening before opening, I was showing the new deck to my close personal friend David Levy. He suggested we put sofas upstairs and a bamboo curtain that could be lowered, allowing total privacy to those who arranged for a private dining experience. I said, "David, we can't do that." He answered, "Why not?" I replied that if we did, there was no telling what would go on up there, and this was still a public family restaurant. His answer was a classic. He retorted, "What the hell do you care as long as they keep sending down for drinks!" Perhaps a good idea, but we never got that far in terms of utilizing the upper deck.

One reason was that the steel spiral staircase we ordered custom made was unfortunately too narrow to maneuver in, especially for our waitresses—certainly when they were carrying large trays of food or drinks.

There was a dance floor installed under the upper deck area. We initially utilized the upper area for live music, with a four-

or five-piece band. I can still hear one of their opening tunes, which blared forth from above, one of the most popular tunes of that time period. It was also one of my favorites: "Tie a Yellow Ribbon Round the Old Oak Tree." We initially thought that having live music was an ingenious way to utilize that upper half roof deck. However, a number of our dancing patrons and lounge customers complained that because they couldn't view the musicians, it felt to them as if the music was "piped in" and not live. Thus we moved the music to the dance floor, using three-piece combos, and the upper area, as neat as it was, was mostly used as a storage area.

To add to our lounge attraction, we hired the best-looking bartender in the Jackson area. She wore white tight shorts and white boots, and could have been a dancer in a "Gentlemen's lounge," had she chosen that profession. As good looking as she was, she also attracted many boyfriends who hung around our lounge, which actually took away from its designed ambience. Also, likely due to a quarrel with one of them, or between two of them, someone set her car afire in our parking lot one evening. That pretty much ended our need for sexy bartenders. Furthermore, we realized that even with the addition of fancy Polynesian drinks, Chinese restaurants mostly attracted family patrons who did not care for any kind of alcoholic drinks, just beer and some wine.

Thus our beautifully designed Polynesian lounge ended up being used for customers who wanted a more private and quieter dining experience than in the main family dining room, and for listening to a band combo on weekends. While some customers did enjoy our bar area and special drinks—that no other establishment in Jackson served—the lounge was never utilized to the extent we had intended it to be. Nevertheless, it did offer a more intimate dining experience for a number of sophisticated patrons who dined out on special occasions. It also offered a quiet meeting environment for businessmen and professionals who needed a place to dine privately.

The Golden Dragon offered patrons in Jackson the only Chinese dining experience in the area for a few years; and the business both expanded and thrived, operating profitably and with enough monetary returns to satisfy several investors. We virtually had a monopoly on serving delicious, authentic Chinese cuisine in Mississippi's capitol city and largest metropolitan area.

And it became the site of my company's weekly sales meetings. Normally, in my Southern Food Brokerage business, we held our sales meetings every Friday. Before the Golden Dragon opened, we would go to Red Lobster for lunch. After the restaurant opened, we would have our business lunch in the Golden Dragon to the delight of everyone except one salesman, who, for whatever reason, did not like Asian cuisine; so Johnny Lee would always cook him fried chicken with rice for lunch.

The Golden Dragon never had to worry about having enough Chinese chefs after the arrival of Johnny Lee. He had several brothers and cousins who worked there with him and filled in whenever we needed extra cooks for special occasions. That was a real relief after experiencing and having to replace the Vanishing Chinese Chefs before Johnny Lee took over the kitchen and general management.

As is normal in a capitalistic society, when a successful monopoly exists, it attracts other businesses of the same nature. After six profitable years, other Chinese restaurants began taking some of our business away. While the Golden Dragon remained the dominant Chinese dining experience in Jackson, the more profitable part of the business had declined to the point that it was not worth the effort anymore. I had organized and overseen the operation from its very beginning without any compensation. Therefore we agreed to sell the entire operation to Johnny Lee for a fair capital gain. He and his family owned and operated that same business for another thirty-five years, moving locations twice. During that time, Johnny had open heart surgery, and still bounced back to continue as head chef and general manager, one who would always come out to the dining room and personally greet every customer. He would always tell them, "I hope you are enjoying what you ordered. If you don't like what you ordered, let me know and I will personally cook something else for you." And he continued to do this until recently when he closed his doors. In his seventies, Johnny and especially his wife felt he had done enough. Now he and his brothers are managing their real estate ventures and ownerships in Hong Kong, which he routinely visits.

15

AFTER THE GOLDEN DRAGON: THE PASTA FACTORY

Being in the food business most of my life from high school through retirement, and having an entrepreneurial spirit, I relished developing a chain of restaurants. Having been in the Chinese restaurant business for six years, the one thing it impressed upon me was that no way could I develop a chain of Chinese restaurants. In order to successfully operate a Chinese restaurant, it must have experienced Chinese chefs. Otherwise a chain of restaurants is close to an impossibility unless the owner-operator is also Chinese, with access to family, friends, and acquaintances skilled in that same endeavor. In that manner, the operation would never be defenseless and always be looking for Chinese chefs during any time of operations. There are a very few such successful Chinese restaurant chains in America, with P. F. Chang's being one of them. Therefore, I turned to another opportunity.

Two of our daughters attended universities near and in St. Louis. Marjie matriculated to the University of Missouri, where she pursued a degree in communications and journalism. The University of Missouri is highly regarded as one of, if not the best, journalism schools in this country. Debbie attended Washington University in St. Louis, highly regarded by many as the "Harvard of the Midwest." She designed her own major in public relations. It must have helped, as she became Miss St. Louis in her senior year. Marjie's major also proved helpful to her as she later became production manager of the highly successful Home Show, starring Gary Collins.

On Sondy's and my many trips to St. Louis, we were impressed with a local restaurant chain known as the Pasta House Company, a successful thirteen-restaurant operation in St. Louis. They featured great and tasty Italian cuisine with a unique wilted lettuce salad. Large portions of various tasty dishes, at reasonable prices in an attractive environment were their specialty. St. Louis has 250,000 residents of Italian heritage. Many live in a certain area known as "The Hill." Some of the greatest Italian restaurants in America are located in that particular section of St. Louis, and most every one of them are family owned. However, the Pasta House Company was different in that it was a small chain, located throughout the city. Therefore, we saw this as an opportunity to replicate the Pasta House Company and bring it to Jackson, expanding it throughout the mid-South.

Initially I sought out and met the owners and inquired about the possibility of purchasing a franchise of their successful operation. While politely receptive, they quoted a price of $250,000 for their first franchise operation. That was far too much for us to even consider at that time. However, in nearby Columbia, Missouri, the home of the University of Missouri (where our daughter Marjie attended), there was a very similar restaurant known as the Pasta Factory, which had been developed and copied after the Pasta House Company in St. Louis. The menu and products were almost identical to the chain in St. Louis. This was the culmination of what we sought.

About a year after we sold the Golden Dragon to Johnny Lee, I spent considerable time, along with an associate, in Columbia, Missouri, studying and copying the Pasta Factory operation, including purchasing its entire recipe and operational book. With that information in hand, I did a six-month feasibility study of the entire operation and possibilities for it in the Jackson metro area. The results appeared positive, and we moved forward from that point.

Some of the same investors in the Golden Dragon were also involved in what we named the Pasta Factory, including Bill Pope, Fred Ray, and Harry Danciger (of egg roll fame). Additional investors were Sondy's parents, Stanley and Rhea Shindell, my mother, Fay Berman, Larry Franck, a highly regarded attorney and dear friend from Ole Miss, and Fred Cohen. Based on the success we had experienced with the Golden Dragon, we anticipated equal or better results with this new venture.

THE PASTA FACTORY LOCATION
AND INTERIOR DESIGN

In 1981, Sondy and I purchased two adjacent homes, which were later moved from a prime piece of property on Lakeland Drive in Jackson to make way for a new commercial building site. It was a cold and dreary day. The two former homes, being utilized as office space, had to be moved without delay so construction crews could install twenty-foot pilings to be placed under the new building. The ground had been frozen, then thawed and turned to mud, making it impossible to move that heavy load up the hill to their new location. The two homes were to be placed on the back part of the parking lot and rented for office space. In order to move the two buildings up the hill and still keep them virtually together, we laid a concrete driveway path up the hill for that purpose.

They were moved the next day and stayed whole. Not even the tiles in the bathrooms were cracked.

In 1982, I had just completed developing a new 36,000-square-feet three-story office building at the eastern entrance to the city of Jackson, on that location on Lakeland

Drive, a major east-west city artery. It had great exposure and accessibility. It was known as the Prudential Building, as the Prudential Insurance Company of America occupied almost the entire second floor. Its name adorned the front of the building in large blue letters, lit on a white building background. There was a large concrete parking lot for tenants and retail space on the ground floor. Off the lobby and two elevators was a 5,000–square-foot area—the perfect location for a major restaurant—that housed the Pasta Factory.

Off the lobby, in front of the restaurant's entrance, was a glassed-in room where our pasta-making machine was located. There we had a chef in white uniform making fresh pasta daily in full view of the restaurant and office patrons. A bank occupied the corner of the ground floor, and Delta Airlines occupied the remainder of the ground floor. My offices for Southern Food Brokerage occupied the third floor. Fred Ray's data management company, SFB's CPA, occupied a large space on the second floor.

As a finishing touch, there was a large pylon on the corner of Lakeland Drive at the main entrance to the property. I had that pylon designed as a fork, with pasta flowing from its prongs.

No enterprise is capable of success without a good and experienced manager and good support staff. A search was initiated in St. Louis, the home city of the Pasta House Company, and among all the superb Italian restaurants on "The Hill." We came upon a young and capable Italian head chef and manager at a country club in that city. After several interviews, we hired him as manager. His name was Vince, and he had a built-in support staff including his wife, his assistant manager, and his assistant manager's wife. Each one had restaurant experience in one form or the other. We moved them to Jackson, Mississippi, and began ordering equipment, furnishings, and supplies.

An interior decorator was employed to design the interior for the best ambience possible. The management staff began interviewing for employees who would be hired and trained as support staff prior to opening.

Sondy and I drove to Atlanta to search for a bar for our lounge. We selected one that was large, long, and perfect for a restaurant bar. We had it shipped to the building and stored until it was installed.

One unique part of the lounge was what we referred to as the Monkey Bar. When we had visited an Italian restaurant chain in Chicago, New York, and Miami, we saw what was one of the most impressive and unique seating arrangements we had ever seen. It was a four-tiered solid brass railing with leather seats interspersed along various parts of the railing. Patrons could easily climb up the various levels to take a seat and sip their drinks. Unfortunately, the Monkey Bar also goes to show that what works in other areas does not necessarily work in Jackson.

We should have recalled that experience from our attempt to emulate Trader Vic's in the Golden Dragon. The great majority of our lounge customers sat elsewhere and only gazed in amazement as some others ventured to climb up and sit at our twenty-foot-high Monkey Bar, of which we were so proud. Not really knowing what to do with it or how to use it, we kept it in place as an architectural design in our overall lounge. Most customers were likely too cautious to climb aboard with a drink or glass of wine in hand, especially with their refill as well. One of the few that enjoyed using the Monkey Bar was myself, hoping that I could entice patrons to join me. That still didn't work.

Another tactic we attempted to attract customers into our lounge was to offer free drinks to the pretty Delta Airline hostesses who frequented the Delta ticket office in our building. It was believed that they would attract male patrons, but the only ones they did attract were other Delta employees.

Finally, our Pasta Factory had hired a full contingent of employees. It was fully staffed, even with backups, beautifully designed, with ground-level tables and booths and second-level (two steps up) seating along the windows with a full line of tables and decorative hanging lamps over each table, designed by a local interior decorator named "Corky." The lounge was on the other side of the restaurant and separated from the eating area by a half wall.

At the entrance from the building lobby, high overhead, was a brilliantly lit and colorful stained-glass canopy. It was designed and built in Dallas, carefully shipped in pieces, reassembled in Jackson, and mounted. No other restaurant in Jackson had anything as attractive or similar to this multicolored stained-glass ceiling entrance.

Just prior to the opening, I assembled our entire crew for a meeting in the main dining room. I stated that I had always wanted to develop a successful restaurant chain, and this was their chance to become a part of that history in a country of great opportunity, right here under the large American flag, which we proudly flew atop the highest point of our building. My hope was that such a pep talk would instill in them a spirit that would last—not just through our opening, but for many years to come.

Even without advertising we opened the restaurant with a bang, as this was the only authentic pasta restaurant in the city. Business was booming. The restaurant had its ups and downs, but mostly sales were great, and it was the "talk of the town." However, after a great opening and overall success for the first year, sales began to taper off.

With such a great beginning, by the end of the first year, overconfidence set in with the manager and his assistant and their wives. They became lackadaisical in maintaining the consistency of the food served and their service and treatment of patrons.

The most important part of any successful restaurant operation is consistency! Consistency in food served, service offered, and ambience. Our management lost control of the first two. The lovely setting and ambience remained the same.

As an example, one evening a United States astronaut and his son, who attended West Point, and their family were dining at the Pasta Factory. After several drinks, they ordered large, family-sized portions of various pasta dishes and some veal for the entire family. After consuming the first orders, they followed up with even more. Apparently one of the pasta dishes was not to the liking of the astronaut, and he called for the head chef to tell him, so that they should not be charged for it. When Vince, the manager, came out of the kitchen to speak with him and heard his complaint, instead of apologizing and offering another similar dish, the manager told him he shouldn't have complained because it was the second helping he had ordered of that same pasta dish. The manager stated, "it must not have been that bad since you ordered it a second time, in an even larger portion."

That response enraged the astronaut—his word was being doubted, especially in public. What happened next was something that is seldom seen in any restaurant establishment. Fortunately it was approaching late evening, around 10:00 P.M., when most customers had finished their meals and had departed the premises.

The astronaut and his son followed the manager into the kitchen and punched him in the nose, knocking him out. Then they paid the bill and departed. That incident so upset the assistant manager that he had to be taken to the emergency room at nearby St. Dominic's Hospital, to be examined and given a sedative. The manager, who had been "coldcocked," had come to and regained his composure. The wives of the manager and assistant manager called me shortly after the incident occurred. I called Bill Pope, a six-foot, four-inch fellow investor to meet me at the establishment. We met about 11:30 P.M. when all had finally quieted down, and the manager's bloody nose had even stopped bleeding. Who were we to believe about the food quality, the manager or the astronaut? That wasn't the primary issue, however. The customer should have been allowed to have his way, to be "right," and his entrée deducted from the bill or replaced with another dish of similar or even greater price—

without charge. But that didn't happen. What did occur resulted in a bloody nose and unnecessary upheaval in the restaurant that evening. It also caused Bill Pope and me to lose some much-needed sleep that night.

OTHER MANAGERIAL PROBLEMS BEGIN TO DEVELOP

From my offices on the third floor above the restaurant, I would occasionally come down during high-traffic business hours to see how the operation was being handled. One day after the lunch-hour rush was finished, I overheard our manager talking over the phone to a potential patron. He said, "Yeah, it will be difficult, but we will try." I asked him "What was that about?" He flippantly replied, "Oh, some tennis team wanted to know if we could accommodate ten couples this Saturday night." I couldn't believe his nonchalant answer. As badly as we needed business, he should have bent over backward to accept them and reserve a space. Ultimately, they went elsewhere, and we lost twenty customers that Saturday night.

Another evening, when I was working late in my third-floor office, I happened to look down from a window in the rear of the building and saw some of our kitchen personnel out back. They were putting some products into our garbage cans, and it didn't look like garbage or trash. I went downstairs and looked into some of those cans. To my amazement, under the garbage were several frozen steaks and lobsters. We were being "robbed blind" by our own crew, and the management claimed they knew nothing about it. Yet they should have!

Management's lackadaisical attitude began to affect our sales as consistency of both product and service started to dwindle. When a restaurant loses its consistency, in any area, especially food, they can go down quickly, and that is what began to happen to our Pasta Factory. We knew we needed a change in management and promptly, if we were to stay in business.

OUR NEW MANAGER—NUMBER TWO

We heard Shoney's had an Italian manager in one of its Jackson restaurants. His name was Jerry. He was a rotund individual in his early forties and sported a mustache. We interviewed him, had him polygraphed, and checked out his references and background to the best of our abilities. He had no criminal record and his references, while not outstanding, proved acceptable. Besides, we didn't have time to search further. We hired him.

The next evening, after the dinner hour, we fired Vince, his assistant, and their wives. It was a bad scene in the restaurant; they had become friends with many of our staff, who became extremely upset, even more so than the management, who were likely expecting to be released. Bill Pope and I stayed around after all personnel had departed to be certain no food was contaminated and nothing was damaged.

The next morning Jerry reported to work bright and early and took command. He was an excellent chef and really knew Italian food because he had grown up on it. He was mature enough to assume control of the staff without any problems, and our business began to level off without any further drop, and eventually we enjoyed some increase.

Jerry changed a few staff members he felt were too close to the previous management team, and the restaurant operations resumed to a far better degree of consistency in every phase.

For the next several months, business began to grow again, and it appeared we could look forward to a brighter future. Then came the Governor's Cup run.

THE GOVERNOR'S CUP RUN

I received a call from Mississippi Governor William Winter's assistant in charge of the Governor's Cup event. He said the governor had chosen our Pasta Factory restaurant for the participants in the run so they could dine on pasta the night prior to the race: pasta is a carbohydrate that boosts the energy level of all the runners. The governor's office would pay for the dinners after they received a final head count. About 500 runners were expected to participate in the run. We were, of course, elated to serve that many patrons in one evening, especially buffet style. We quoted a reasonable price per adult person, reduced for children.

Since a portion of our third floor was not fully occupied at the time—and we had two elevators—we decided to utilize that area plus the entire 5,000-square-foot restaurant area to feed all those runners. We closed the restaurant to other patrons that particular evening.

All preparations were made, including pastas, sauces, cheese, salads, bread, nonalcoholic drinks, tables and chairs upstairs, and buffet tables up and down, with chafing dishes beneath the food trays to keep the buffet foods hot and tasty. Jerry was assigned to manage the downstairs, and his wife was assigned the upstairs.

All of a sudden the rush started, and we were inundated with hundreds of hungry runners and their families. Hostesses were stationed in the building lobby entrance to guide the patrons either downstairs or to the third floor via the elevators. Signs were also there to help direct the customers.

The evening started off great. However, some time after the flood of customers began entering, there was no sign of Jerry. I kept asking, "Where is Jerry?" and finally someone told me that Jerry was in the freezer making a beautiful ice carving for the governor. That would have been great, except that the governor and his wife had been among the first to arrive and had long since left the premises. Jerry was needed out front! I finally found him, still carving an impressive block of ice he had turned into a sculptured runner, which would have been terrific had it been done hours earlier. But that was not to be.

Furthermore, as I went upstairs, I noticed that the flames to heat and keep the buffet items hot were mostly extinguished. I took it upon myself to get on my knees, crawl between patrons under the line of tables, and relight the heaters. That wasn't a dapper thing to do, but it had to be done!

One other item of interest about that night was the note left for me by the governor. It said, "Bob, thanks for a great evening. All our runners had an enjoyable meal and will surely be ready for the race tomorrow. I am leaving a $50 tip for your servers who did a good job." It was signed "William" (Governor William Winter) and looked like his handwriting. However, there was no $50 attached.

I thought, *what a nice gesture* by the governor. The next morning I called the governor, thanked him for staging the "pasta feast" the night before at our Pasta Factory, and also told him how much I appreciated the $50 tip he had left for our servers. For a moment there was dead silence. Then he replied in amazement, "I left no such tip, even though it was a nice evening and handled well by your staff." That was somewhat embarrassing to me. I explained that it must have been a ruse by someone and regretted bothering him. He merely laughed about it and we hung up. That was no joke to me!

CRASHING THROUGH OUR LOBBY

One evening about 9:00 P.M., I received a call that an SUV had backed up and crashed through the glass enclosure of our main building into our lobby. It literally destroyed half the lobby leading to the restaurant's entrance.

Fortunately, the only thing that stopped it from also entering the inside dining room walls was the metal and concrete stairwell that divided the lobby from the restaurant itself.

What had occurred was this: the driver had been drinking at our bar prior to leaving. When she backed out of her parking space, she must have lost control and completely twirled around and backed full steam into our lobby—and all the way through it.

As an aside, on the lobby wall next to the staircase was a cigarette machine. Earlier we had decided to limit access to cigarette smoking in our building and restaurant establishment. A week earlier I had called a friend, Ronnie Lott (now president of the Rotary Club of Jackson), who owned the machine and asked that he remove it. A week later, I called him to forget about the removal since the SUV had backed directly into it and crushed it to smithereens. Even the cigarettes were completely destroyed.

THINGS START GOING DOWNHILL AGAIN

For whatever reason, our daily sales began to falter again. Perhaps one reason was that a couple of new Italian restaurants had come to the city, and new restaurants always attract an initial rush of customers. The other reason was that Jerry apparently had some family problems. He was not devoting as much time as needed to the details of managing our large restaurant to ensure its continued success. Our investors therefore recognized that the time was rapidly approaching to once again change management.

However, more was needed than just a new manager. As much as our new pasta establishment for Jackson was accepted by the public, it appeared that if we were to remain in business, an entirely new concept was needed.

A BRIEF INTERLUDE AND A
HORRIFYING DISCOVERY

During the brief transitional period prior to changing management for the third time, I was supervising the luncheon and dinner meals. One noon, when the restaurant was crowded with an overflow of patrons, I noticed a customer who caught my eye from the upper seating area near the windows. He recognized I was part of management and quietly motioned to me. I stepped up the stairs and walked over to his table for two. Once there he proceeded to point downward to his large chef's salad. I was aghast at what I saw.

In the middle of his salad, as if topping it off, was a large, half-dead cockroach. Before the salad came out of the kitchen and was served, it must have been under the lettuce. Fortunately, before the customer put his fork into the salad, it must have found its way to the top. This wasn't a small bug; it was one of those Mississippi cockroaches with wings that, had he been fully alive, probably could have put the salad on his back and flown off with it to one of the surrounding pine trees where they nest. I immediately swooped up the plate from the table, profusely apologized, and on my way to the kitchen, asked over my shoulder, "Can I get you anything else?"

I couldn't believe his reply. He responded, "Yes, just bring me another salad." What a considerate and courageous gentleman he was. I would have expected him to quickly depart the restaurant and never return. Thankfully he didn't scream when he discovered the large bug.

I usually do not raise my voice when I am that exasperated, but I had a difficult time restraining myself as I approached the head luncheon chef. After showing him the plate, I asked how in the world could anything like that occur, when we routinely have our entire premises treated for pest control and pride ourselves in keeping our kitchen so immaculate. He replied that just before lunch the pest control service man came in and sprayed the kitchen area, and the cockroaches came scrambling out from the cracks in the walls and elsewhere. I told him if he ever allowed that to happen again, he not only would be immediately fired, but be blacklisted in other restaurants in the area.

Thankfully that was the only time something like that, or anything resembling it, occurred during the three years we owned our restaurant. We did change the pest control company, as they should have known far better than to spray during business hours. It should have been anathema to them.

THE BIRTH OF "VICTOR'S"

In our search for a new manager, we knew of an excellent chef that was also managing a successful, small local restaurant owned by his wife's mother. We approached him and offered him 50 percent ownership in our restaurant at its present location—if he accepted the head chef and management responsibilities of a new concept we intended to mutually develop, with continental cuisine and some unique specialty foods. Since our restaurant had a beautiful ambience and was so well located, with modern décor and relatively new equipment, he accepted our offer. A new menu was designed featuring the new cuisine, yet keeping a few popular pasta dishes. We heavily advertised the new concept and the name of the new manager. He was well known and respected in the area, and the patrons quickly accepted him. The food was superb, and our business began to soar.

For the next year, business boomed, and so did our profits. However, and unfortunately, once again it was not to last.

One day I walked into our kitchen and found a big Labrador retriever lying on the floor next to one of the stoves. While it appeared well kept and well groomed, I asked our manager to whom it belonged, and he replied it was his. I said, "We cannot have a dog or any other animal in our kitchen, or any other place in our establishment." He said he always brought him to his mother-in-law's restaurant. I told him to keep it there and not in our place. That irked him, but I didn't care. It was absurd to allow a dog or any other animal on our premises, especially where the food was prepared!

Even though our management owned half the business and its profits, due to the manager's lack of attention and absence at times, our restaurant business began to falter. Apparently, it was assumed, our business was directly affecting his mother-in-law's business (located not far from our restaurant) and customer traffic. Instead of patronizing her place, customers came to a much nicer and more attractive environment for the same cuisines and prices, prepared by its former chef. That likely took a toll on the manager's desire to give Victor's the close attention it not only needed, but deserved, to continue its success.

A FINAL MANAGEMENT CHANGE

We recognized, once again, this (third) management change also wouldn't work, even though, without question, it should have considering the manager's capabilities, and his ownership of 50 percent of the profits. Additionally, negotiating with him to surrender his stock ownership, which we had given to him at the beginning of his employment, was ticklish and required careful handling. I left it to our CPA and one of our owners, Fred Ray, with whom the manager had no problems, to negotiate the return of our company stock and to dismiss him. Fred was successful with that delicate assignment.

THEN WHAT!?

I was determined not to let our business completely die, especially with all the money we had invested in its location, equipment, interior design, and business to date. So what to do?!

When we lived in the Mississippi Delta twenty-five years prior, we frequented a very popular steak house known as Doe's Eat Place. It was in a shabby part of the town of Greenville, in a former house, and patrons would eat in the kitchen and the connecting rooms. All Doe's served were steaks, hot tamales, French fried potatoes, onion rings, and salads. Alcoholic beverages had to be hand carried. Doe's was known all over the South for their delicious steaks. Most do not know the secret of how the steaks are prepared. I asked and was shown.

They cook their steaks on ovens specially built just for that purpose. The steaks are cooked by gas flames from the top of the oven. The only ingredient they put on their steaks before cooking is salt. As the steaks are cooking, they take the drippings from the fat and meat and continually baste the steaks with the drippings, giving them that "extra" flavor.

A first cousin of mine, Richard Lewis, formerly of Indianola, Mississippi and now of Atlanta, took that method to that large Southern city and opened a steak house in the Buckhead area. The restaurant is known as Bones, and for the past thirty years it has been the most successful and leading steak house in that entire metro area.

I ordered two of those special ovens and intended to turn our restaurant into a steak house similar to Doe's—except for the environment. I tried to persuade one of the members of the Doe family to come to Jackson and manage and own the restaurant with us, but to no avail.

IN THE "NICK" OF TIME

Then one day I received a call from a real estate developer, Pete Apostle, who had a young cousin who wanted to return to Jackson and open his own Greek restaurant. His name was and is Nick Apostle. He was part of a family of restaurateurs who owned several establishments. He was managing one for the family in Little Rock, Arkansas. He had graduated from Millsaps, a fine, well-known private liberal arts college in Jackson, and his lovely wife Alice had graduated from Ole Miss. They missed their Mississippi relatives and friends, and were looking for an opportunity to relocate and have their own establishment in the Jackson metro market. Nick's father owned a successful, family-style restaurant in Jackson, on the other side of the city, known as Paul's.

After several meetings and negotiations with Nick, and after consulting with our owners, we agreed to sell our restaurant "lock, stock, and barrel" to Nick. He purchased everything we owned, including the merchandise, the equipment, and the fixtures as is. He also paid us our full asking price, which showed what a fine individual he was and continues to be. He and his wife renamed the premises *Nick's.*

Nick and his wife Alice made a huge success with his white-tablecloth restaurant serving continental cuisine. They did it in the very same location, with mostly the same equipment, décor, and personnel.

He did eliminate the Monkey Bar and long Pizza Conveyor Belt machine in our kitchen, where we were the first restaurant to make a variety of deep dish pizzas, introducing them to the Jackson area in the Pasta Factory. He also eliminated the pasta-making equipment that we used to make our own pasta. He had a beautiful luxury-style lounge and expanded with two private dining rooms, which he needed for private parties.

So, people do make a difference! Where we initially brought in an experienced restaurant management team of Italian heritage from St. Louis, then switched to an Italian chef who had managed a local Shoney's restaurant, and finally changed to and employed a top-of-the-line, experienced chef from his mother-in-law's local kitchen—none of them, for a variety of reasons, could make a lasting success out of our fantastic location. Nick and Alice did, overwhelmingly, with Nick's!

For almost thirty years Nick ran a highly successful dining establishment at this location, and he was one of the major tenants in our building. His restaurant was also known as one of the best in the entire state. A few years ago, long after we had sold the building, for whatever reason, Nick moved to another location, with an entirely new style restaurant and bar.

Our building and the adjacent properties we had acquired over the years successfully sold in 2003 to a local investor and to the Baptist Hospital. It is now owned by a former mayor of Jackson and his son.

OVERCOMING ADVERSITY

Throughout my years of owning Southern Food Brokerage, the Prudential office building, shopping centers, and restaurants, I overcame two embezzlements decades apart, a necessary major managerial change of a key company executive, and a real estate meltdown, some of which were simultaneous. While at the Harvard Business School, George Baker, another one of my professors and a future dean of the school always stressed, "Concentrate on your strengths and eliminate your weaknesses." That I did, along with adhering to one of my favorite expressions: "If you ever want to achieve success at anything in life, you must stay everlastingly at it."

PART V

PRODUCTION TIME

16

MY TIME AS A PRODUCER—
AND MY IN-HOUSE SUCCESSOR

In my earlier years in Jackson, I also started a side venture as a producer of entertainment in the metro area. While at Lewis Grocer company and Sunflower Food stores, during my first full-time position in the food industry, I was assigned the responsibility of organizing a large food show at the new state Mississippi Coliseum on the Mississippi State Fairgrounds in Jackson. It was a major undertaking, as I had to contact almost every supplier of food and beverage products carried by the company—and then sell them on the idea of paying for a booth and advertising their products in one or more booths at our upcoming food show, which I had named the "Foodarama." It was the first major show ever held in the Coliseum, and attracted a huge crowd, both customers and the general public.

To attract a large audience for such a show, I knew that we would need a well-known and popular entertainer or group to do their act throughout the Foodarama. I chose and booked the Four Aces, one of the country's leading musical groups at that time. Some of their most popular tunes were "Three Coins in a

Fountain," which was featured in a romantic movie of the same name, "Shangri-La," and many others. They were a big hit with the crowd and also helped attract people to the entire food show.

Later, for Sunflower Food Stores' annual conventions, I booked such well-known entertainers as the Grand Ole Opry's Minnie Pearl, singing star Vaughn Monroe, movie and singing star Gloria DeHaven, and others.

As a matter of fact, since those acts were such big hits and relatively easy to book, and the nationally known entertainers such a joy to associate with, once we moved to Jackson several years later, that success encouraged me to take on another side venture. I became a producer of big shows in the Coliseum and in the relatively new and beautiful Jackson Auditorium.

While I met with a reasonable degree of success, producing taught me a good lesson. What one can book, pay for, and bring in to a "captive audience" is decidedly different from entering into ventures that need to attract sizable general audiences, if the return on time and investment is going to be worth the risk.

THE KIDS NEXT DOOR

During a visit to Jackson, Bob Hope, perhaps the finest all American comedian and entertainer that ever lived, was featured at the annual arts show in the Mississippi Coliseum. In his show, he happened to pick a young lady from the audience (most likely preselected) to come on stage and sing with him. She performed well, and the audience liked her. Afterward she joined a new national singing group known as The Kids Next Door.

Since she had appeared locally with Bob Hope, I believed that if well advertised and publicized, The Kids Next Door, featuring this young lady, would be well received in the Jackson market. Thus I booked them for one evening to appear in the 2,500-seat auditorium.

The night prior to the performance, Sondy and I invited

the young singer to our home for hamburgers cooked on our grill. We had a nice chatty evening together. In those days, prior to the ultimately successful civil rights movement, no African Americans had ever appeared with Caucasians on stage in Jackson, especially not in dance scenes with male and female partners. While such an event would never have bothered us, it was anathema to a good number of the local population. Before leaving the singer casually mentioned that her group now had a great black dance partner that should wow the audience. In other words, we were going to be the first to break the color barrier on stage in Jackson. Irrespective of the fact that it should not have even been a problem, we nevertheless wondered how it would be received. We did not need to wonder for long.

The next morning, the day of the performance, I notified our master of ceremonies, who was an outstanding humorist and also a preacher at a Baptist church in the Mississippi Delta, about the circumstances of that evening's performance. His job was to introduce each act and to have one of his own between the song and dance routines.

He was aghast and immediately said he could not appear on the same stage with blacks and whites dancing and singing together. What a predicament that was for me. It was like "being on my sled three miles out of Anchorage, and my lead dog dropped dead."

I knew I had to do something quick to resolve the situation, so I contacted my friend and attorney Larry Franck, and asked his opinion; I had a contract for the MC to perform. He recommended meeting with him and attempting to convince the MC/preacher that he was only a hired part of the show, not the producer. I did that, and the first thing he told me was if he appeared on that show, his congregation would ride him out of town on a totem pole, if not tar and feather him. Finally I was able to cajole him into going forward with the show, but only if during his act, as he demanded, the lights in the auditorium were raised. What a strange request. But we did not even question it and did just that, which pacified him. The show went on as planned. It received a good review in the daily newspaper. Nothing whatsoever was mentioned about public interracial dancing, which had been entirely proper, as it should have been. No one in the modest crowd that attended seemed to object in the least bit. The auditorium was almost half full, and the gate income just paid for the performers and other expenses. In other words, it could have been seen as a break-even event that unexpectedly broke the color barrier on stage in Jackson, Mississippi. That it was, and that it did.

However, I was not to be denied bringing in a truly successful entertainment show to the Jackson metro market.

THE MONKEES

A friend of mine and I noted that The Monkees were a hot item at concerts, and they even had a TV series. He also was interested in promoting shows in Jackson. Although we had competing food brokerage companies, we nevertheless respected one another and decided to book The Monkees for a show in the 9,300-seat Coliseum. They were quite expensive, in addition to the state fees to book the Coliseum and advertising costs.

By the day of the performance, we had not sold enough tickets to break-even. That evening, however, busloads of fans came in and put us over the top into a profit position.

Some hours before show time, my partner received a call from one of The Monkees asking for eighteen tickets to the show. He asked what for, and they said they had met some girls on the street and wanted to get them in free. My partner objected strenuously and told them we were paying them a large guarantee, and tickets were made to be sold, not given away. They responded, "If you don't send us those tickets, we won't show!" My partner finally relented and sent ten tickets up to their room, and that apparently satisfied them, as we met them backstage about two hours before show time. They were in their dressing room preparing for the show.

The red light came on, there was a knock at their door by the stage manager who said, "You're on in five minutes." They completed their prep, came out of their "Star" dressing room door, stood in a circle with their arms around one another's shoulders, and began enthusiastically jumping up and down, similar to the way football players do just after coming out of the tunnel and onto the field. When they went onto the stage, they were really pumped up and ready to put on a great show— and that they did.

The more than 5,000 fans in the crowd went wild with enthusiasm, screaming, stomping the floor, clapping their hands, and swaying from side to side. It was an exciting night for all in attendance.

While we didn't make a big profit from that evening's take, it was enough to continue my interest in the field of promoting, until I received two long-distance calls within a couple of months of each other.

GLEN CAMPBELL AND TOM JONES

Several months after The Monkees show, I received a call from an agent who said, "I've got a great act for you to bring to Jackson. He is replacing The Smothers Brothers show on TV this summer and is available for you to book this fall." I had watched the Smothers Brothers and knew they were popular, but what about their summer replacement? I asked his name, and the agent replied, "Glen Campbell." My response was just the opposite of what a cagey producer would have said. I replied, "I don't think I want to book him, because if I do, by the time fall comes around, his TV show could be a flop and I would have a 'dead horse' on my hands." Thus I refused to book him, and when he later performed in Jackson, there was standing room only in the 9,300-seat Coliseum (and Sondy and I were among those standing up and applauding). What a miscalculation, where I could have made a bundle on the show and become friends with a great future star.

My father used to say, "It's not a fool that makes a mistake, it's a fool that makes the same mistake twice," and that I did when I received a call from another agent out of Shreveport, Louisiana, who offered me an up-and-coming new star—none other than Tom Jones. Once again I made the same mistake and turned him down.

MY IN-HOUSE SUCCESSOR
AND THE METROPOLITAN OPERA GREATS

After the Glen Campbell and Tom Jones fiascos, I decided it best not to continue pursuing a side venture career as a producer.

However, I happened to have a successor in my immediate family, and that was my wife, Sondy. She was president of the Mississippi Opera Guild, whose parent organization was The Mississippi Opera Association, one of the oldest opera companies in America. They had the skills and knack for choosing the best voices possible and brought them in to perform on stage in the well-designed new City Auditorium.

Their organization sought out and booked the very top opera stars in the entire country to perform in Jackson, along with other opera stars and local talents. Among those greats were Jan Peerce, Robert Merrill, Beverly Sills, and Richard Tucker, with whom Sondy performed on stage in *Aida*. During that performance she wore a beautiful tiara, and I must say she looked magnificent. During the week Jan Peerce was performing, we had him for dinner at our home in Jackson. Sondy's parents, Rhea and Stanley Shindell, were there for the dinner and performance. The meal had to be specially prepared as Peerce ate only kosher, but he must have enjoyed it as he left nothing on his plate.

Richard Tucker required all the air conditioning turned off, as he felt it affected his voice. They were allowed to keep the auditorium fans running. Beverly Sills sat on a chair backstage in the doorway of her dressing room and munched on an apple between acts. She was extremely friendly with Sondy and the entire cast.

Each of the operas the Opera Association booked was a huge success, filling the 2,500-seat auditorium with sellout crowds.

PART VI

CHASING RAINBOWS

The previous sections of this book have been the "Beyond" portion of *Chasing Rainbows and Beyond*. Parts VI and VII begin and conclude with the "Rainbows" I have been chasing, and are by far the most important and compelling chapters—especially my "Final Four."

17

ALWAYS CHASING RAINBOWS

From the time I left Harvard and began working at my grandfather's wholesale and retail supermarket chain, there were some major ventures that I planned and investigated, but which never came to fruition. I always recalled the expression, trite as it may be, "If you reach for the stars, you will never get mud on your hands." Additionally, I believed in Robert Kennedy's words when he said, "Some people see things as they are and ask why. I dream of things that have never been and ask, why not."

Even though some major "dreams" I chased that had the potential for large financial gain never materialized, it was the joy of the research and feasibility studies I did, and the sheer possibility of success that made them so exciting and interesting to me and worth chasing.

They were shared with me by one of the most intelligent, successful, and honorable businessmen and humanitarians I have ever known. He also believed each dream had merit. His name was Earle F. Jones. He and his lovely wife, Irene, were "backyard neighbors" of ours for thirty years in Jackson, Mississippi.

Earle graduated from UCLA, and later from the Harvard Business School, prior to my graduation from that institution. Afterward, he and his wife moved from their home in California to Jackson, at the request of his partner, Mike Sturdevant, who owned some of the first Holiday Inns and had been a classmate of Earle at Harvard. Earle was summoned to help share the management of their hotel development company, and they were highly successful together. They also owned and operated the King and Prince, a resort on St. Simons Island off the Georgia coast. Earle was chairman of the Mississippi Management Corporation. He was also chairman of the Starwood Corporation when their Sheraton Hotels owned and operated casinos in Vegas and elsewhere.

He was the best friend and associate I could have ever wanted to have join me in our efforts to achieve financial success in the major projects I describe below—with the exception of the first one, where we were on opposite ends of the spectrum. Each of these endeavors took place prior to my personal and most important Final Four humanitarian projects described in the last section of this book, entitled "Hope." They were and still are the "Rainbows" most worth chasing!

A MAJOR TELEVISION STATION

This chase I made did reach a "pot of gold" at the end of its "Rainbow." Earle and I happened to be on opposite sides of this venture, as he represented the Federal Trade Commission (FTC) and I was one of the subsequent investors.

An NBC affiliate, WLBT, the largest television station in the Mississippi marketing area, was cited by the FTC for discrimination against members of the black community. Because of that, it had its license revoked.

Due to his outstanding reputation, Earle Jones was chosen by the FTC and named chairman of a holding company for the station until a new licensee could be named.

Bob Travis was a highly respected attorney in Jackson. He was also a good friend of mine. One day I received a call from him asking if I would be interested in joining a small group of investors that were seeking to be the new owners of WLBT. The initial investment was relatively small. After hearing the details, some of which I was familiar with, I agreed to become one of the investors.

Each potential investor was thoroughly vetted for the FTC by the FBI prior to being allowed to become one of the new owners. They even talked with my rabbi, Richard Birnholz, about my character. Afterward he asked me, "What's going on with you and the FBI?" I know there are a total of 613 commandments in the Old Testament of the holy Bible. However, since I must have passed the "Top Ten," I was allowed to join our group of potential investors. We were competing with more than one other group of investors for the ownership of that valuable TV station. Eventually we merged with one of the other groups, and after a considerable period of time our new multiracial group was allowed to become the new owners of the prized WLBT station.

One of the employees of that station was a man by the name of Woody Assaf, their weatherman, who was also a longtime friend of mine. After we were awarded the new license, he must have been the one who arranged to have my picture placed on the wall of that station, along with the new manager and a few executives of the station, although I had nothing to do with the station's day-to-day management. The photo must have remained there until we eventually voted to sell the station to a large investment firm.

Without disclosing the overall details of the sale, I can reveal that for that initial trivial investment, I received an extraordinarily large bonanza and net return on my investment, reaching six figures. While it took ten years from the time I joined that investment group until I received my final share of the sale, that was one rainbow definitely worth chasing!

CAT ISLAND

While working at Lewis Grocer and Sunflower Food Stores, I utilized my spare time in planning a development of a barrier island off the Mississippi Gulf Coast. It was the only such island that was privately owned and is situated just seven miles off shore. It is twenty-six miles long and four miles wide, with nineteen miles of natural, sugary white sand beaches. I made a feasibility study of the possibility of the State of Mississippi building a causeway to the island, connecting it directly to State Highway 90, which runs along the entire beach area of the Mississippi Gulf Coast.

On that island, I proposed building a state-owned casino, similar to the one at Monte Carlo in Monaco (in Europe), with profits used to support the state treasury, especially education. I made a number of trips to that island to explore it. The island's owner took me out on the first trip. Additionally, I had a single-engine plane and pilot fly me over the island for about an hour while I took close-up pictures of the beaches and interior. Prior to taking off, while waiting for the pilot, I noticed some loose rivets on the wing of the plane. I questioned him about it when he arrived. He responded, "Nothing to worry about," as they were secure enough and wouldn't fall off. I took him at his word and am still here and able to write about it.

In my first nonfiction book, published by Quail Ridge Press in 1988 and titled *More Than Survival,* my story was featured as "One Man's Plan to Move Mississippi Forward in the 21st Century." One of my recommendations was for the state to put into effect my plan for Cat Island, including the state-owned casino project, among several other plans to fund the state treasury.

At the time, as was true frequently in the past, our state was hurting financially in its need to support education and other major necessary services. It had the lowest per capita income in the country and was struggling to survive. Yet, growing up in that environment, I knew the people of Mississippi were strong and capable, deserving much more than mere survival. Thus, from that belief came the title of my book.

Some people believed that bringing gaming into Mississippi was heresy. Mississippi has more churches than any other state and a large Baptist population. Gambling at that time was mainly confined to Las Vegas and Atlantic City. Nevertheless, I personally placed a copy of my book on the desk of every state legislator. I cannot take credit for what transpired four years later, but the state legislature approved gaming for the State of Mississippi, one of the few states in this country that did so at that time. Since then, gaming, tightly controlled, brings in approximately $200 million to the state treasury and half that amount again to the cities and counties where gaming is allowed. At least my book and its recommendations caught someone's eye—or more than one someone who had the authority to make a difference.

After my book was published, I was interviewed by Bert Case, news editor at WLBT, the NBC television affiliate in Jackson. He asked me if I thought my book would really generate any changes for the better in our state. My answer to him was to repeat what John Kennedy once said: "One man can make a difference, and every man should try."

Some years later, even after gaming had been approved by our state legislature, my good friend and cohort, Earle Jones, and I still felt that Cat Island had potential for some type of resort development, with all of its white sand beaches and especially since it had surf; the Mississippi Gulf Coast in contrast has none since it is protected by several barrier islands. We leased a helicopter and flew out to the island and landed on the sand beach. The helicopter ride to and from the island was somewhat treacherous because the copter had only two seats—for the pilot and one passenger; thus I held on to the open door and Earle on the way out, with my feet hanging over the Gulf waters 100 feet below (and he did likewise on the way back). Once we landed we explored the beaches and interior, and I went for a swim in the surf.

Prior to personally touring the island, we had contacted the children of the original owner, who had since passed away. We arranged to meet with them in their offices the next day in New Orleans, only sixty miles away. At the meeting we discussed with them the possibilities of developing the island, either with or without a causeway, as a resort venture, showing them our plans for its development. We met with their entire family. After due consideration they decided it was in their best interest to take an offer from the Federal government to purchase the island from them as a Federal land reserve, similar to the other barrier islands off the Mississippi coast, while setting aside a small portion of it for a privately owned family beachfront home. That was a sure thing for them; our plan was not.

A CASINO FOR JACKSON, MISSISSIPPI

While the state had legalized gaming, it had done so in certain areas only. They were on the water, from the Mississippi Gulf Coast, along the Mississippi River up through Natchez, Vicksburg, Greenville, and Tunica.

This plan did not reserve a place along the interior Pearl River waterway for at least one such casino in Jackson, the state's capitol.

Earle and I felt that was a most unfair oversight to the people of Jackson and Hinds County, as the income, ad valorem, and sales tax would have been significant to that area also. We had the architectural group of Godfrey and Bassett design a meticulous plan for a $250 million casino and high rise hotel, river walk with shops and restaurants, convention center, and 5,000 seat amphitheater entertainment complex on the Pearl River, which would have connected to the Coliseum and State Fairgrounds, next to downtown. This development would have been an extension and expansion of the downtown area and could have helped revive a downtown that had begun to deteriorate. It would have provided an estimated 3,100 jobs. The plans made headlines in the Jackson *Clarion Ledger* daily newspaper, with full-page color details, and stirred considerable excitement among the populous.

HOLLYWOOD CASINO

Because of Earle's position as chairman of Starwood, and his relationship with the Holiday Inn hotel chain, he was acquainted with the owners of the Hollywood Casino group, which owned the Sands Hotels and others. We flew to their luxurious headquarters in Dallas and presented our plan to them. Their offices were atop a high-rise hotel, and another elevator was required to reach their penthouse headquarters. They were quite impressed and agreed to come to Jackson to further explore the idea. The Deposit Guaranty Bank offered us their large meeting room for Hollywood's presentation in connection with ours. It was attended by a number of influential members of the community, city officials, and state legislators. It appeared Hollywood was prepared to make a proposal to the Mississippi Gaming Commission to be allowed to become the one and only casino in the Jackson metro area, on the riverbank, as we had designed it. What a bonanza that would have been for the city. If legislative approval could have been attained, the only other obstacle was the fact that the mayor and city council were reluctant to grant an exclusive casino to the investors.

FOILED BY THE FICKLE FINGER OF FATE

After our meeting, a casino convention was held in Las Vegas the following week. Somehow, some way, the owners of Hollywood were made an offer they couldn't refuse, to drop their plans for Jackson. It was surmised that they had either been offered substantial monies to drop their bid for a Jackson casino, or had been threatened with being blacklisted in some manner in the casino industry if they tried to override the originally planned locations for casinos in Mississippi. Hollywood dropped the idea like a hot potato. Perhaps another reason Hollywood decided not to pursue was because of the city's refusal to grant them the right to an exclusive casino, if ever approved by the legislature. Thus our 250 million dollar offer to the city was withdrawn.

A CASINO FOR JACKSON: PLAN TWO

Not to be outdone by the Hollywood group, I developed another casino plan for Jackson, and Earle felt it also had merit and went along with the idea.

We designed a plan to have the three casinos in nearby Vicksburg jointly own the one new casino in Jackson, in the same development we had planned along the Pearl River bank next to downtown.

To offset any loss of business they might experience from the casino in Jackson, we planned to take over an abandoned railway line between Jackson and Vicksburg and set up a special, privately owned train service between the two cities—from the Jackson airport to the Jackson casino and then on to Vicksburg and its casinos. The train would also service all the large, undeveloped land tracts between the two cities for major new real estate developments. It was a grand design.

MEETING BETWEEN JACKSON AND VICKSBURG CITY OFFICIALS

We set up an important meeting between the mayors of Jackson and Vicksburg, as well as some officials from both cities. We proposed that they allow us to implement that development plan with the three casinos in their city. The PowerPoint presentation went as scheduled, and after we answered several questions, was well received. However, that grand plan also never got off the ground because the Vicksburg mayor was reluctant to approach the casinos in his city for that purpose.

A few months afterward, I happened to meet the newly elected mayor of Vicksburg at the Jackson International Airport. I briefly told him what had transpired and about our grandly designed plan. He immediately felt it had merit and asked us to represent it to him and his city council.

About that same time, Earle and I were investigating another potential entrepreneurial venture in the food business that likely had a much better chance of success and wouldn't take nearly the time and effort it would have taken us to re-pursue our casino plan for Jackson. Thus, that was the end of that plan.

PANERA BREAD

Several years ago, the Panera Bread Company was a relatively new, up-and-coming restaurant chain featuring a large assortment of breads, desserts, and sandwiches. J. D. Powers gave it a very high rating.

Earle Jones and I each had envisioned developing and owning a chain of successful restaurants through the country. So we did a feasibility study of Panera. I had several discussions with their director of development, invested in their stock on the Exchange, and attended their annual stockholders' meeting in St. Louis. I met its president and other corporate executives.

We initially wanted to develop stores within our own state of Mississippi. However, there were only two markets large enough to attract Panera's corporate image and requirements. In order to purchase a Panera franchise, one had to agree to develop a minimum of fifteen stores, each requiring an approximate million-dollar investment. This also had to be finalized within a certain amount of time or the initial units would need to be sold to the parent company at a precalculated figure. We had planned to open one or two at a time, and then parlay the cash flow from those units to supplement the investment needed for the next units to be opened, until we reached our goal of fifteen units.

We visited several Panera restaurants, primarily in the California area (formerly Earle's home area), between Los Angeles and Santa Barbara, spoke with their managers, and checked them out as thoroughly as possible. That is the area we chose to develop in, and it was available. We met with the president of Lowe, in Los Angeles, to review the area and its best potential sites. What we discovered was that the cost of property in that part of California, even undeveloped, was prohibitive. We would have needed to leverage our investment funds to the extent that the cash flow for the first several years would not have been sufficient to utilize for helping to open new units. Thus we abandoned the California area and looked elsewhere.

Panera was still not ready to open in the Jackson area. We looked at Memphis, which could have been ideal, and we met with the original owners and founders of Corky's Barbecue chain. While initially quite interested, however, they felt that entering into a partnership for Panera restaurants in their area would not be profitable enough, considering Panera's heavy franchise fees and requirement to develop and own fifteen units within a certain period of time.

Our dream of owning a chain of Panera restaurants could have still materialized. Their management offered to sell us the ownership of the Alabama Panera Restaurants. After we researched it and met with some of the Panera personnel, we observed that some of those Paneras, while well located and attracting good business, had not met with large success profit wise. We would have needed to struggle for some time to bring them up to par, including making more of an investment than if we had opened them ourselves. So we passed on that offer by

Panera's management, and that was the end of our interest in that company.

In actuality, as good as it looked initially, we were most fortunate we did not get involved with opening Panera restaurants anywhere at that time, as shortly afterward, in 2008, just as we would have begun reaping intended profits from the ones we had opened, the worst ever recession hit, almost to the extent of becoming a depression like the one of the 1930s. With the obligation to continue opening new units until our quota of fifteen had been reached, we really would have been behind the eight ball on this project. Thus, after all of that effort, we were fortunate that it ended the way it did.

PART VII

HOPE: MY FINAL FOUR

Orison Swett Marden once wrote: "There is no medicine like hope, no incentive so great, and no tonic so powerful as expectation of something [better] tomorrow."

My "final four" were ambitious humanitarian projects that I envisioned and strove to achieve. They are noted last, because even though I was never able to complete them, I believe the embers they contain remain alive. Each one in itself could make a difference for good in the lives of so many.

They were the "rainbows" truly worth chasing—and they still are.

None of the projects were designed to benefit myself or my family, either financially or otherwise. They were planned for the sheer purpose of benefiting society as a whole, in our state of Mississippi, in our nation, and in certain other parts of the world.

John F. Kennedy, in his presidential inaugural address on January 20, 1961, most eloquently, with wisdom and keen perception, said, "With a good conscience our only sure reward, with history the final judge of our deeds, let us go forth to lead the land we love, asking his blessing and help, but knowing that here on earth, God's work must truly be our own."

So in reality, it must be. God gave us this life. Now it's up to us, not God, to do his work here on earth—to make this world a better place in which we all can share and live together peacefully with dignity, justice, and compassion.

18

THE HOPE SCHOLARSHIP

In our global society and today's economy, the better our youth are educated, the more successfully our country can compete with other nations throughout the world. The more successfully we compete, the more enhanced will be the lives of our citizens.

The state of Georgia for many years has offered a Hope scholarship to all of its high school seniors. Georgia's Hope scholarship is available to Georgia residents who have demonstrated academic achievement. The scholarship provides money to assist students with the educational costs of attending a Hope-eligible college in Georgia.

Simply stated, a Hope scholarship is available to any high school student who graduates from a Hope-eligible high school with a 3.0 (B) grade point average.

Once they enroll in one of Georgia's universities or other eligible colleges, they must continue to maintain a 3.0 grade point average in order to continue attending and receiving a free college education at that academic institution. The scholarship can be applied to a four-year college or a two-year community vocational college. Such a scholarship serves as an inspiration to each and every student to strive for academic excellence.

The Georgia Hope scholarship plan deserves to be emulated by any state that can muster the continuing financial resources to provide every one of its high school students a free college education.

When I received the honor of becoming a district governor of Rotary International, I had one primary goal for my term. That was to bring hope for a better future to the children of Mississippi.

In my initial address to the Rotary district assembly, I stated and explained that "hope for the children of Mississippi" was my primary goal for the year I would serve as Rotary governor. What a great opportunity to give every high school student in Mississippi the hope and real possibility of receiving a free college education. All they needed to do was achieve and maintain a B grade point average.

One of my responsibilities as Rotary district governor was to travel to all forty-four clubs in the district and address their 2,500 members. On each such occasion, while I stressed the importance of Rotary and its many opportunities for service, I stressed my theme of a Hope scholarship. My wife Sondy accompanied me on almost every visit.

The Rotary committee I assigned this effort was asked to project the maximum number of students that would be eligible to receive this free education and the cost. The state was already offering a free college education to those who attained a B+ average. Thus those students were not included in the additional amount necessary to fund all those other achievers holding between a B and a B+ average.

The maximum amount, if all eligible high school students achieved and accepted a Hope scholarship was projected to cost the state approximately $50 million per year. That amounted to less than 1 percent of the state's annual budget. Such an expenditure would have opened the door for a free college education to any and all high school students within the state. It would have further helped keep the best and brightest students within Mississippi's seven state universities.

Among our committee members, there were three in particular that come to mind who worked so very closely with me to accomplish this important goal. They were Louis Watson, a highly regarded attorney in one of the state's leading law firms, Joe Dove, a highly regarded staff writer for the Jackson daily newspaper the *Clarion Ledger,* and J. Walter Michel, a senator in the Mississippi state legislature.

We assiduously met several times with key state legislators, including the chairman of the appropriations committee. He personally stated that most every day when he opened his mail, there would be a letter from me urging passage of legislation to support a Hope scholarship for Mississippi. We also attended a meeting with the chancellor of the University of Mississippi and all the other presidents of each state university and received their endorsements—including a personal letter of support to me from the then-chancellor of the University of Mississippi, Dr. Robert Khayat.

While Rotary International is not a political organization, it does seek to improve the lives of all youth. Without question, we were operating within the purview of one of Rotary's missions.

As diligently as we worked throughout the year, and even though we had the legislation to accomplish that mission placed into the legislature docket by Senator Walter Michel, with a companion bill in the House, it was never brought out of committee for a vote. The lawmakers claimed the funds would not be available consistently on an annual basis.

The state of Georgia funds its Hope scholarship from funds received through a state lottery, and it has done so for many years. It is considered so vital that it has become a part of the Georgia Constitution. Mississippi has no such lottery. However, Mississippi does have something Georgia does not, and that is legalized gaming, with a multiplicity of casinos from the Mississippi Gulf Coast and up the Mississippi River to just below Memphis, Tennessee. Our Rotary year was finished before we could take our efforts in this matter further, and it was not part of the plan of the Rotary governor who succeeded me.

Mississippi's casinos would likely oppose adding a lottery within the state as they would feel it would add competition. However, the casinos in Mississippi have one of the lowest tax bases compared to almost any other state in which they operate. That is one of the key reasons the state has been so successful in attracting all the casino investments it has. Mississippi has more casino square footage than any other state in the nation, other than Nevada and New Jersey.

The state's casinos would be a way to help fund the Hope scholarship in Mississippi as the lottery does in Georgia. It certainly would be a way to improve the image of the casinos in the minds of the public, especially those people who still oppose gambling in any form.

A realistic plan of action would be for the state to first ask the casinos to jointly fund it, as the lottery does in Georgia. By dividing the amount among all the casinos in the state, that would appear to be feasible and not present an undue burden on any one of them.

If that was not acceptable, the state could offer to fund one-half of the amount needed to implement a Hope scholarship in Mississippi if the casinos would defray the other half on a continuing basis. Since inflation has been relatively low and controlled over the past decade, the $50 million we projected would still be close to realistic. Even if the total had increased a small amount, it would still be reasonable to pursue the idea of the state funding $25 to $30 million annually and the casinos funding the other half. And look what it could achieve, for the state and for its most prized possessions—its youth! This goal unquestionably is achievable if there are enough forward-thinking legislators to see its merit.

With the extraordinarily high cost of college tuition today, the Hope scholarship would be a godsend to the majority of students, not just in Mississippi, but unquestionably to the students in every other state of this great country.

19

HOPE FOR STARVING CHILDREN

As wealthy and prosperous as our great nation is, there remain children within our own country who go to bed hungry most every night. This is a continuing problem that needs to be strongly addressed from a humanitarian standpoint by our state legislatures and the legislative and executive branches of our nation. It must not be overlooked and allowed to continue!

What is even more a stain on humanity are the children who are actually starving to death in various parts of our world, in Africa in particular.

Rotary International, where I am a past district governor as mentioned earlier, is the first international civic organization in the world dedicated to service. (It was founded in 1905.) It has over 1.2 million members in more than 60 countries with over 30,000 Clubs. It is secular, nonsectarian, nonpartisan, and nonpolitical.

Rotary International has five areas of service:

- **Club Service** focuses on making clubs strong, enabling them to function successfully.
- **Community Service** encourages Rotarians to find ways to improve the quality of life for people in their communities and to serve the public interest.
- **Vocational Service** calls on Rotarians to work with integrity and contribute their expertise to the problems and needs of society.
- **International Service** exemplifies Rotary's global reach in promoting understanding, goodwill, and peace.
- **New Generations Service** (Youth Service) recognizes the importance of empowering youth and young professionals through education and leadership development. They are the future of Rotary and the world.

Rotary International's continuing major goal is known as Polio Plus, launched in 1985 to rid the world of polio. The only other disease that has ever been eradicated worldwide is small pox. Rotary has accomplished 99 percent of its Polio Plus goal: reducing the number of children paralyzed worldwide every year by polio from 350,000 in 1979 to 223 in 2012. More than 2.5 billion children have been immunized against polio. Working as partners with the World Health Organization, the U.S. Centers for Disease Control and Prevention, and UNICEF, Rotary International raised over $1.2 billion for that purpose.

Its members and spouses actually go into the hinterlands to administer the polio vaccine to the children of each country, many times risking their lives. In 2009 half the world's polio cases were in India; today there are none! There remain only three endemic countries where polio has not been eliminated. They are Afghanistan, Nigeria, and Pakistan. Some tribal leadership may fear these vaccinations are a Western attempt to poison their children. Just as dangerous are Islamist militants who claim that polio vaccine campaigns are a cover for Western espionage. They have frequently attacked health workers and their security teams.

Unfortunately there are those in these backward nations that lack the education, knowledge, and/or the intelligence and desire to accept this life-saving immunity for their youth. Until poliovirus transmission ends in these countries, *all* countries remain vulnerable to importation of the polio virus, especially in the countries from west Africa to the Horn of Africa. Nevertheless, Rotary is dedicated to completing the task, and it is so very close. Bill Gates and Melinda Gates have been so impressed with Rotary's efforts in this campaign that their foundation has contributed $1.9 billion to Rotary to help this cause. Since UNICEF and the World Health Organization are among the partners of Rotary in this life-saving cause, it appears they should take the lead in alleviating the fears of those in the three polio-endemic countries, assuring them that this is not a Western plot, but a global initiative to save the lives or prevent the crippling of their children. The same applies for the United Nations itself.

Eliminating hunger is another Rotary goal. Saving starving children fits into that category. According to the Rotary Trustees' Chair of 2013, almost 2.6 million children die each year from malnutrition.

My wife, Sondy, and I have attended twelve Rotary International conventions around the globe. At one of those conventions, I came upon a display booth that was manned by a nonprofit organization known as Breedlove Foods, Inc. This company in Lubbock, Texas, partly utilizes the abundant produce of the region coupled with a state-of-the-art commercial-sized food dehydration plant to provide tasty and nutritious dehydrated soups and vegetable blends for various organizations that serve the most vulnerable throughout the United States and around the world. Breedlove was established in 1994 by the South Plains Food Bank of Lubbock, Texas.

Prior to that, the South Plains food bank would, on occasion, receive bulk loads of produce from area farmers or a Frito Lay plant that operated in Lubbock during that time. That plant occasionally rejected a load of potatoes that would not produce the quality and color of potato chip required, but the potatoes were fundamentally sound. The food bank was unable to handle the storage and distribution of loads this size, so much of the produce would spoil and be wasted. Breedlove was created as a way to effectively process and utilize the potatoes. They have refined the formulation and packaging of the product over the years, but the basic approach since that time has changed little. The product has since been used in over eighty countries worldwide in much the same fashion as it was in the early years. To date they have delivered well over one billion servings and have built the capacity to deliver an even greater volume in the future. Breedlove became its own separate 501(c)(3) charitable nonprofit organization with proven success.

Literally for pennies per serving, Breedlove food products are being used to feed starving children and adults, and they are making a difference for hundreds of thousands of poor and needy people of all ages throughout the world.

But it can do more, especially throughout the continent of Africa, where there are more starving children than anywhere else. At a cost of less than ten cents per serving, Breedlove Foods offers solutions for feeding the hungry and saving the starving. One truckload of dehydrated soup is the equivalent of seven truckloads of fresh or canned food. Dehydrated foods require no special refrigeration or storage. One forty-foot overseas cargo container of Breedlove dehydrated soups or vegetables holds roughly one million servings. At most, the shipping cost of sending dehydrated food anywhere in the world will add a couple of pennies per serving.

In 1997, a group of Rotary International officers, including President Glen W. Kinross, President-elect James Lacy, and Foundation Chairman Clifford Dochterman, visited the Breedlove Foods' plant in Lubbock, Texas. They examined the product and were apparently impressed with its potential to save the starving, as noted by the words of Glen W. Kinross in his

"President's Message" in *Rotary World* (May 1998, Vol. 4, No. 5, p. 2) as follows:

> Among the many hunger-alleviation projects now under way is a Rotary-sponsored dehydration plant that I visited in Lubbock, Texas, U.S.A. This facility had the capacity to produce 500,000 pounds of dehydrated food per week—that's 10 million servings. Think about what this one Rotary project could mean to some of the millions who go to bed hungry every night of their lives.

Over a decade later, in late 2011 and early 2012, I assembled a multidistrict group from several Rotary districts in the United States, including Lubbock, Texas; Jackson, Mississippi; Oxford, Mississippi; Los Angeles, California; and Boca Raton, Florida, to pledge $33,000 plus (including $28,494 for cost of food and $4,600 for cost of transportation) to ship one twenty-foot container of vegetable-blend, chicken-flavored product to Kenya to feed the starving men, women, and especially children from Somalia in the Kenya refugee camps. This would have resulted in a cost per serving of .064 cents.

I was working through District Governor Eric Kimani, of Rotary District 9200 (of which Kenya is a part), and also Paula Lanco-Mutua, who was one of the district leaders helping to coordinate relief efforts in their area.

We were aware that Rotary International was collecting and distributing funds for relief projects in the region through its "Horn of Africa Relief Fund." However, by working directly through Breedlove under their district's control, our method appeared to be a way of feeding a large number of needy children and others at a minimal cost, and hopefully in an expeditious manner.

Prior to finalizing this humanitarian aid, we needed written approval of and full cooperation from District 9200.

That included their agreeing to pay all fees at the port of entry, arranging and paying for the transportation to the feeding site, and arranging and paying for storage until all product was consumed. Additionally, they needed to be fully responsible for the security and safety of the product and its distribution directly to the needy in the refugee camps.

Past Rotary International president Frank Devlyn was aware of our attempts to save those starving in Kenya, and kindly wrote me the following on January 10, 2012:

> Dear Bob:
>
> Good you are trying to help Kenya with dehydrated food for those in need. I am copying PDG Yusuf Kodwavwala who might also be able to help.
>
> Your amigo in Mexico City,
> Frank Devlyn

This humanitarian project to save the starving in Kenya fell apart at that point, as Rotary District 9200 did not provide the written guarantees needed for us to proceed with our plans.

Perhaps they either could not or would not provide the guarantees necessary to help feed the starving souls in their refugee camps. However, I am confident Rotary International does have the power, the organizational skills, and the funds through grants to utilize Breedlove products to save so many, many starving people in that area of the world and beyond.

Therefore, I am sending a personal copy of this book to my friend and immediate past-president of Rotary International, Ron D. Burton, with a recommendation that Rotary International take up the cause, through Breedlove, that can save the many lives of those starving in that part of the world. His theme for 2012–2014 was "Engage Rotary, Change Lives." This surely is a project that can achieve just that! After his term as president, he is due to become trustee chair of the Rotary Foundation, which provides such funds through its grant program. The following information is from Breedlove's website:

> Recent statistics indicate that approximately 840 million people in the world don't receive adequate nutrition to maintain health. In short, they are starving to death. Particularly disturbing is the fact that around 30 thousand of these die unnecessarily each and every day from a hunger-related disease, with a large portion being women and young children. That's more than AIDS, malaria and tuberculosis combined. The unfortunate truth is that millions more will continue to succumb to this misfortune in coming years. . . . Breedlove Foods is able to develop and produce nutritious products for distribution around the world for those most vulnerable, and at a reasonably low cost.[11]

Let's start saving these lives by working through a company like Breedlove Foods. If Rotary International gets involved, many of these lives can unquestionably be saved.

---

11 http://breedlove.org/index.php?option=com_content&view=section& layout=blog&id=3&Itemid=37

20

HOPE FOR TOLERANCE

O ne of the world's greatest needs is that of tolerance—
the ability to respect, honor, and dignify the rights and
beliefs of others, as long as they do not trespass upon
the rights of others with their different beliefs and customs.

MUSEUM AND HOUSE OF TOLERANCE:
THE UNIVERSITY OF MISSISSIPPI

My second book, *A House of David in the Land of Jesus,* was
all about tolerance in one of the least expected places, the rural
Mississippi town of Lexington, where I grew up. It was a true
story, a history of goodness, where Christians and Jews, blacks
and whites all worked together for the benefit of the entire
community.

In 1905 my grandfather Morris Lewis, along with his
brother-in-law Sam Herrman, donated the land for and built the
synagogue named Temple Beth El. It celebrated its centennial on
December 2nd and 3rd, 2005. Rabbi David Ellenson, president

of the Hebrew Union College, attended and gave the keynote addresses at each service; one at Beth Israel Congregation in Jackson and the next morning at Temple Beth El in Lexington. Membership at Temple Beth El dropped from its peak of eighty-nine Jewish souls in the late 1930s, just before World War II to only twelve families in 2005. In his talk, Rabbi Ellenson compared those twelve to the twelve tribes of Israel.

Those twelve families were not enough to support that synagogue, even with membership from elsewhere—that is, our family and others. Therefore I recommended in my book that the temple, with its eight beautiful stained-glass windows—or a replica of the building with its windows—be donated to the University of Mississippi in Oxford, to be converted into a center and museum of tolerance. It would not only relate the great story of tolerance in Lexington, but also tell the story of slavery, the Civil Rights movement, the Holocaust, and the horrific results of intolerance. A classroom set up in that venue would also teach tolerance, and what can obviously happen when the opposite is present.

The tolerance center was to be located on campus on an attractive piece of real estate on University Avenue, at the main entrance to the University and adjacent to the impressive Gertrude Ford Center for the Performing Arts. It would be the first major building that all would see as they entered the University—a symbol of tolerance, justice, and peace.

My wife, Sondy, and I met several times with the Chancellor, Dan Jones. He was not only receptive to the idea, but initially stated he would lead the drive to fund it.

The University was going to send an architect to inspect the stained-glass windows to determine if they were indeed movable. As time went on, nothing transpired. Finally the chancellor related to me that the Board of Trustees for the State Institutions of Higher Learning would be reluctant to approve any project of that kind until it was presented to them with the $5 million estimated to build the center.

Even though the center was to teach tolerance among all the great religions of the world, it nevertheless came about from one particular religious source. This might not have been acceptable to all. Recognizing this fact, I reorganized and enlarged the plan on a strictly secular basis. An exhibit focusing on 9/11—as another example of the tragic results of intolerance—was also added to the exhibits for slavery, civil rights and the Holocaust. The classroom was also expanded to accommodate over 100 students.

The expanded museum would have required approximately $10 million to build. I offered to lead the drive to obtain those funds, with the support of the Chancellor. However, once again the Chancellor felt the Board of the State Institutions of Higher Learning would not consider it without the available monies, or at least a major portion of it.

That was the last contact I had with the chancellor about that project. However, the plan is still in place, and the embers of the proposal continue to flicker. Perhaps someday, some soul with access to one or more major charitable funds will be captivated by the idea, and it will then become a reality. If so, it would be the only such "Center and Museum of Tolerance" at any state-supported university in America, and would become a tribute to the university, to Mississippi, and to humanity overall. The teaching of tolerance at that site would be what is needed not only in Mississippi, but in this great country of ours, and throughout this small planet.

Ole Miss has only two statues on its campus. The first one stands at the entrance to the university and is that of a Confederate soldier. It is in memory of all those young male students who left college to fight for what they believed was the right cause at that time. None of them survived to return. Through Abraham Lincoln's strength and tenacity in holding the Union together, that cause proved fallacious. A much more recent statue was added by the university, in another well-located site near the library. That statue is of James Meridith, honoring his courage as the first African American to enter and enroll in the university and commemorating the integration of the races at Ole Miss. This statue was a public commitment by the university to openly honor tolerance and the importance of the God-given rights of every human being.

The dire need for more tolerance never becomes outdated. With that in mind, Benjamin Netanyahu, Prime Minister of Israel, stated, "We should never be tolerant of intolerance," which seeks to destroy the very values tolerance brings to this world. Consider the Holocaust and its horrible results; the worst example ever of human's inhumanity to other humans. And the hate of 9/11 that resulted in the largest loss of life through one act our country has ever sustained; and the injustice of slavery and racial inequality; and we must never overlook the dangers of radical Islam and the jihadists who seek, through force, to convert the entire world to Islam and a caliphate under its Sharia law (Islamic law, as opposed to democratic and constitutional law). Remember, appeasement never works; just ask the "ghost" of Neville Chamberlain. Beware. Beware!

21

HOPE FOR A CURE—FOR ALS (LOU GEHRIG'S DISEASE)

Unfortunately, one of our dear daughters, Marjie Berman Block, was diagnosed with amyotrophic lateral sclerosis (ALS or Lou Gehrig's disease) in 2009. She is a beautiful young mother of three boys and has the fighting spirit of Winston Churchill, who believed in never giving up, never, ever! If anyone can beat this horrific disease, Marjie will be one of the first to do so. "ALS is the most vicious of all afflictions," according to James P. Bennett, Jr. M.D., Ph.D., ALS physician-scientist.

The remainder of my life on this earth is devoted to helping find a cure for ALS, which would not only save Marjie's life but the lives of 30,000 other Americans afflicted with this terrible disease and the 5,000 new cases diagnosed each year. The cause of the dreaded disease is unknown. To date, it is incurable. The average life span after diagnosis is two to five years, but there are others who have outlived this average. In layman's terms, the disease destroys the motor neurons of the brain and spinal cord, which control the muscles in the body. Without those neurons, the muscles atrophy and are unable to function, eventually including muscles that control the lungs and the ability to breathe.

Prior to Marjie's marriage, she worked for Ted Turner at TBS in Atlanta, followed by directing public relations for the Miss Universe organization, traveling worldwide. Her last position was as production manager of television's *Home Show* starring Gary Collins in Los Angeles. Besides devoting herself to raising her three boys and being a loving wife, Marjie was president of the PTA. She also made a dramatic effort to help the victims of Hurricane Katrina when it swept across the Mississippi Gulf Coast. From her home in California, she single-handedly arranged for an eighteen-wheeler truck with a fully loaded trailer of food and clothing supplies to travel to the Gulf Coast—even before FEMA arrived. For this effort, she received the humanitarian award of the year from her Temple Menorah and a certificate of appreciation from the County of Los Angeles.

Marjie has written many meaningful poems during her lifetime. While battling this terrible disease, she wrote the following:

Don't be afraid of me.
Don't be afraid to be alone with me.
Don't be afraid to join me in outings.
Don't be afraid to invite me out to join you.
Don't be afraid to walk with me.
Don't be afraid to talk with me.
Don't be afraid to ask me to repeat myself.
Don't be afraid to ask what I need.
Don't be afraid to ask what I want.
Don't be afraid to ask if you should lend a hand.
Don't be afraid to talk about the illness.
Don't be afraid to talk in seriousness.
Don't be afraid to ask questions.
Don't be afraid to share new insights.
Don't be afraid to offer creative ideas.
Don't be afraid to give gentle reminders.

Don't be afraid to joke around and laugh.
Don't be afraid to have fun with me.
Don't be afraid to reminisce with me.
Don't be afraid to join me in adventures.
Don't be afraid to enjoy life with me.
Don't be afraid to be my friend.
Don't be afraid to let me be your friend.
Don't be afraid to touch me.
Don't be afraid to hug me.
Don't be afraid to love me.
I'm still here, I'm still me.
Don't be afraid.

—Marjie Berman Block

AWARENESS IS IMPORTANT—RESEARCH IS VITAL

Awareness is important, as too few citizens of this country even know anything about this terrible disease unless it is referred to as Lou Gehrig's disease (after whom it is named). Lou Gehrig was the renowned New York Yankee's first baseman who died of ALS at the age of thirty-seven in 1941. His famous farewell speech to baseball, and his many fans at a day honoring him at Yankee Stadium in 1939, is still remembered today.

A Hollywood movie depicting his life and career titled *The Pride of the Yankees* was featured in 1942. It starred the great actor Gary Cooper (as Lou Gehrig), along with Teresa Wright and another baseball legend, Babe Ruth himself, who was a close friend and teammate of Gehrig. It's worth viewing, even today.

However, unless awareness results in dollars devoted specifically for ALS research, awareness is in vain. Awareness alone will not help find a cure for ALS; research dollars will!

Research efforts can be threefold:

209

1. Increasing a patient's function while he or she remains alive;
2. Stopping the progression of ALS—changing it from a "fatal" to a "chronic" disease that can be kept in remission until a cure is discovered. This in itself would be a remarkable achievement. That is currently the stated goal of Dr. Jonathan Glass, Chairman of Neurology and head of the current ALS stem-cell trial at Emory University in Atlanta.
3. Finding a cure for ALS—the ultimate goal.

Once these goals are accomplished, it is most important to note that the same approach could possibly be utilized to cure other major neurological diseases, including multiple sclerosis, Parkinson's disease, and even Alzheimer's disease.

ALS DRUGS AND OTHER THERAPIES: FEW AND FAR BETWEEN

The only ALS drug that has been approved by the FDA thus far is Rilutek (riluzole), which helps to increase life span by a mere three months. However, today, nearly seventy-five years after Lou Gehrig died of this disease, there are finally some encouraging possibilities for attacking and conquering ALS. They are primarily related to a few promising drugs not yet approved by the FDA, and stem-cell and genetic therapies.

ALS Drug Therapies

These are the drugs that are currently or soon to be in human clinical trials.

R(+)Pramipexole

Dr. James P. Bennett, professor and department head of the department of neurology at Virginia Commonwealth University, discovered a drug known as R(+)Pramipexole. He did a successful trial of that drug, and later it was tested in Phase I and Phase II trials by Knopp Biosciences. For its Phase III trials, Biogen, a biotechnology firm, purchased it from Knopp. While the drug was proven safe, Biogen later abandoned their Phase III trial as it did not meet their expectations for efficacy. That was regrettable as some who are continuing to use the drug in a much smaller study have shown a slowing of the progression of the disease. In 2013, Knopp attempted to take control of the drug from Biogen and reignite their research of its potential. However, Tom Petzinger, Knopp's executive vice president, confirmed in a phone conversation with me that there is no longer any litigation. Knopp is continuing to research R(+) Pramipexole and plans for additional trials, either repeating their successful Phase II or taking it into a larger trial.

Currently, Stephen and Barbara Byer, owners of ALS Worldwide, have the rights to continue their trial of this drug and are making it available to those who believe it can help them, but at a steep price due to the cost of the drug.

Nuedexta

According to Avinar Pharmaceutical's website:

> Nuedexta is the first and only FDA-approved treatment for pseudobulbar affect (PBA) [a condition that occurs secondary to a variety of otherwise unrelated neurological conditions]. PBA is characterized by involuntary, sudden, and frequent episodes of laughing and/or crying. These episodes typically occur out of proportion or incongruent to the patient's underlying

emotional state. Studies to support the effectiveness of Nuedexta were performed in patients with . . . ALS and multiple sclerosis (MS). . . . In the STAR pivotal clinical trial, the primary outcome measure, number of laughing and crying episodes, was significantly lower in patients treated with Nuedexta compared with placebo. The secondary outcome measure, the Center for Neurologic Studies-Lability Scale (CNS-LS) [a measurement of rapidly changing emotions], demonstrated a significantly greater reduction in the mean CNS-LS score from baseline for the Nuedexta-treated patients compared with placebo.[12]

This included the ability of patients with ALS to actually improve, including speech function. According to Dr. Merit Cudkowicz, there is an ongoing trial, led by Dr. Richard Smith, to address this very question.

Gilenya

"Made by Novartis, this fungal derivative locks up T cells in the lymph nodes and prevents them from circulating. Already approved for multiple sclerosis, Gilenya increased survival in ALS mice by a week—a meaningful amount given the severity of the model . . ." according to Dr. Steve Perrin, CEO and Chief Scientific Officer of the ALS-Therapy Development Institute (ALS-TDI). A Phase IIa safety trial was completed in late 2014, with results expected in the Spring of 2015.[13]

Genervon Biopharmaceuticals LLC

Genervon's novel, proprietary, multitargeted biological drug candidate, GM604, shows significant promise for treating ALS.

---

12 http://www.avanir.com/nudexta
13 http://www.alzforum.org/news/conference-coverage/chicago-als-clinical-trials-new-hope-after-phase-3-setbacks

On October 19, 2014, the company announced the results of their Phase IIa trial of GM604 after completing its analysis of its double blinded, randomized, placebo controlled clinical trials of ALS and Parkinson's disease for its drug candidate GM6 (GM604).

The two trials were designed to determine whether a six-dose treatment of GM6 would begin the process of disease modification. Even though a small trial, the clinical and biomarker data in the ALS trial reported statistically significant results.

GM604 significantly reduced the decline in ALSFRS-R versus the historical control, p=0.0047. Seven out of eight treated patients had their ALS disease progression slowed or stopped at week 12 after initial six doses of GM604.

Five out of seven treated patients had their forced air capacity disease progression slowed down or reversed at week 12 when comparing with historical placebo.

The results also suggested GM604 was shown to be safe and tolerable when delivered intravenously. It should be noted that such results quoted are from a press release, not from a scientific, peer-reviewed journal.

Genervon has received both fast track and orphan drug designations for GM604 in the treatment of ALS. It has submitted the positive and encouraging results of these trials to the FDA for guidance on how to make GM6 available as a therapeutic for ALS now, even prior to the long and tedious process of a Phase III trial. Irrespective, in the interim, Genervon is planning the next trial for GM604. Genervon intends to partner with one or more pharmaceutical companies in connection with this effort." [14]

Neuraltus Pharmaceuticals, Inc.

Neuraltus Pharmaceuticals, Inc., is a privately held biopharmaceutical company developing novel therapeutics to treat neurological disorders. The principal Investigator is Dr.

14   http://www.genervon.com/genervon/about_pressreleasestxt.php

Robert G. Miller, director of the Forbes Norris MDA/ALS Research and Treatment Center of the California Pacific Medical Center. Study efficacy results have demonstrated positive trends in the ability of NP001 to slow the rate of disease.

NP001 is a small molecule regulator of inflammatory macrophage activity. Aberrant macrophage activity is believed to be a significant contributor to the pathology underlying ALS. Neuraltus' NP001 is designed to restore the normal functioning of macrophages within the central nervous system.

On September 1, 2014:

> Neuraltus Pharmaceuticals, Inc. announced [...] promising efficacy results of the Company's Phase 2 clinical program of NP001 for the treatment of amyotrophic lateral sclerosis (ALS, or Lou Gehrig's disease) [...]. According to a post hoc analysis administration of a high dose of NP001 (2mg/kg) was associated with a halt in disease progression in 27% of patients, approximately 2.5 times greater than the percentage in patients on placebo (10%). The researchers determined that two major plasma factors— Interleukin-18 (IL-18) and lipopolysaccharide (LPS), both markers of inflammation—may differentiate NP001 responders from non-responders.

> In the analysis, the responder population was shown to have had significantly higher levels of IL-18, a cytokine involved in inflammation-driven cell death, than the non-responders at baseline (p=0.02). Additionally, all NP001 responders had detectable levels of LPS in their plasma, signifying abnormal macrophage function, whereas none of the placebo non-progressors had detectable LPS at baseline.

> Neuraltus Founder and Chief Scientific Officer Dr. Mike McGrath, [...] commented, "We are excited by these results, which to our knowledge provide

the first evidence of a more favorable response to an investigational ALS clinical candidate based on the patient's own immune status. [...] We believe that elevated IL-18 and the presence of LPS, both of which indicate an ongoing neuroinflammatory process, may help identify patients more likely to benefit from NP001. Blood markers such as these may become an important tool in helping identify potential treatments for different subpopulations in this heterogeneous disorder." Based on the current clinical evidence, Neuraltus expects to initiate dosing in its next clinical trial of NP001 in the second quarter of 2015.[15]

Other potential ALS drugs

In attempting to list potential ALS drugs presently in trials and those being considered, fortunately the field has begun to quicken, and this book is being written at a "moving target." Dr. Merit Cudkowicz, director of neurology at Massachusetts General Hospital in Boston, has named two additional ALS drugs currently starting in trials. They are retigabine and inosine.

Retigabine is used as an adjunctive treatment for partial epilepsies in treatment-experienced adult patients.[16] Inosine is a chemical that can be made in a laboratory and is used as medicine. People take inosine for improving their athletic performance. There is information that suggests inosine might help nerve branches (axons) grow from healthy nerves to injured nerve cells in the brain and spinal cord, but more research is needed.[17]

For further information on the latest therapies, visit the NEALS consortium site at www.alsconsortium.org and www. clinicaltrials.gov.

---

15 http://prnewswire.com/news-releases/neuraltus-pharmaceuticals-als-treatment-candidate-np001-highlighted-at-als-research-group-summit-275419691.html

16 Molar Mass: 303.331 g\mol http://en.wikipedia.org/wiki/Retigabine

17 http://www.webmd.com/vitamins-supplements/ingredientmono-704-inosine.aspx?activeingredientid=704&activeingredientname=inosine

ALS Stem-Cell Therapies

One of the most encouraging possibilities in the fight against ALS has come about with the use of stem cells.

Neuralstem

At this time, stem cells therapies are a real possibility. Neuralstem's Phase I trial was completed at Emory University under the auspices of world-renowned neurologist and site principle investigator Dr. Jonathan Glass. The head principal investigator is Dr. Eva Feldman at the University of Michigan, where they have combined with Emory and Mass General in Boston for Phase II of this ALS stem cell trial, which is now complete. This procedure takes the commercially produced neural stem cells from an eight-week-old fetus and injects these cells directly into the grey matter of the opened spinal cord in both the lumbar and cervical regions. While it does not produce new motor neurons that connect to the muscles, it does produce astrocytes (glia cells that help protect and support neurons) that in turn produce GDNF (glial cell line-derived neurotrophic factor), a protein that surrounds and protects those motor neurons that remain alive and also theoretically nourishes the sick ones back to good health. They are referred to, in short, as neurotrophic factor, proteins responsible for the growth and survival of new neurons and the health of mature neurons. Unique to Neuralstem's technology is their ability to also create neurons that integrate with the host's remaining motor neurons, and the "delivery" of medicine is more potent that way.

Dr. Nick Boulis, associate professor of neurosurgery at Emory, was the surgeon for all of the Phase I surgeries. He is the inventor of the spinal-mounted stabilization and injection platform and floating cannula surgical devices used to deliver the cells. The device floats up and down with the patient's breathing, allowing it to accurately inject the cells.

"The completion of this Phase I study is a major milestone for the testing of intraspinal stem cell therapy for ALS," said Jonathan Glass, MD, professor of neurology and pathology at Emory University School of Medicine and director of the Emory ALS Center. "We have now shown that the procedure is safe for both lumbar and cervical injections, allowing us to move forward with an aggressive program to test whether this treatment will improve the course of disease for patients with ALS."[18]

On September 22, 2014 Neuralstem, Inc. announced:

Jonathan D. Glass, MD, site investigator at Emory University, presented long-term follow up data on the Phase I trial testing NSI-566 human neural stem cells in the treatment of [ALS]. The presentation, which occurred at the Annual symposium on ALS of the Foundation Andre-Delambre, in Montreal, Canada, . . . and was not open to the public, covered data up to approximately 1200 days post the stem cell treatment.

Dr. Glass reported that patients in the last safety cohort [in Phase I], who received treatments in both the lumbar and the cervical region with the highest number of cells per injection, all showed significant slowing of the progression of the disease. One patient showed functional improvement from pre-treatment baseline, which is maintained to present day. The other two patients are maintaining the same level of functionality as they had at the baseline for over three years since the stem cell treatment. . . ."The long-term follow up data is very encouraging," said Karl Johe, PhD, Neuralstem's Chairman and Chief Scientific Officer. "In Phase I, patients 10, 11 and 12 each received 10 lumbar and five

18 http://investor.neuralstem.com/2014-03-17-Final-Results-Of-Neuralstem-Phase-I-Stem-Cell-Trial-In-Amyotrophic-Lateral-Sclerosis-Published-In-Annals-of-Neurology

cervical injections, of 100,000 cells each, which was far below the safe maximal dose. Even so, the data shows a significant slowing of the disease progression for over three years. If replicated on a larger scale, this could represent meaningful improvement in quality of life, and lifespan, compared to untreated patients. In our Phase II dose escalation trial, we successfully reached the maximal dose planned, which consisted of 20 lumbar and 20 cervical injections of 400,000 cells each, more than ten times the number of stem cells delivered in the highest dose cohort of the Phase I trial."

"The progress in this trial is truly groundbreaking," said Dr. Glass, who is Director of the Emory ALS Center at Emory University, the first site in the trial. "It has provided data on the safety of multiple injections and multiple transplantation surgeries in ALS patients as well as the long-term survival of the transplanted cells in the human spinal cord. This provides a strong foundation for moving ahead with more definitive trials focused on the potential therapeutic efficacy of spinal cord transplantation of neural stem cells for ALS."[19]

In Phase II, Groups 1 through 4 received cervical surgery. The cervical area (neck) is the most important for living since it affects breathing and swallowing. The fifth group had cervical surgery next, and then one month later this same group had lumbar surgery. There were eighteen surgeries in all in this Phase II trial. These surgeries, which have now been completed, are followed by a six-month observation period, after which a "data lock" report will be submitted to the FDA.

Once approved by the FDA, then Phase III trials are planned to begin in 2015; they will test the safest maximum therapeutic dose for efficacy.

---

19 http://investor.neuralstem.com/2014-09-22-Neuralstem-ALS-Investigator-Presents-Long-Term-Follow-Up-Phase-I-Data

Neuralstem, Inc. (NYSE MKT: CUR) is the company that produces and grows the neural stem cells. Its president and CEO is Richard Garr.

With Colorado's recently passed "right-to-try" law, patients in the state with terminal diseases can test out therapies yet to receive FDA approval. Neuralstem plans to make its treatment for ALS available in Colorado.

At this time, the company has yet to decide whether it will charge for the stem cell therapy, but it is already in the process of training Colorado surgeons on how to administer the treatment that requires special equipment and a considerable amount of skill. In a Phase I study published in *Annals of Neurology* this year, implantation of Neuralstem's human spinal cord stem cells proved to be safe. According to Colorado's new law, that is all that's necessary to offer the treatment to ALS sufferers in the state.[20]

BrainStorm

Hadassah Hospital in Jerusalem, Israel, is testing an ALS stem-cell program. It is now in its Phase IIb trial. They have named this procedure NurOwn, their proprietary, first-of-its-kind technology for the propagation and differentiation of autologous mesenchymal stem cells into a neurotrophic factor that secretes cells and their transplantation at or near the site of damaged motor neurons. A patient's stem cells are harvested from their bone marrow and then grown and treated in a petri dish to differentiate them. Afterward, when injected into the patient's spinal fluid and muscles, they can surround the motor neurons with astrocytes (as in the Neuralstem therapy), nourishing those motor neurons that remain back to health and protecting the others. An article from Hadassah, titled "FDA Approves US Clinical Trials to Treat ALS with Israel Stem Cell Technology," reports:

---

20 I. Richard Garr, CEO, Neuralstem, Inc.

Earlier clinical trials at Hadassah have shown that the treatment was both well tolerated and safe. "Ten of the 15 patients in the Hadassah trials responded or stabilized," reports Prof. [Dimitrios] Karussis, [who heads the trial] "and the disease was halted, with their breathing improved. About three of them even showed that the disease had receded, with them improving dramatically." He notes, however, that the treatment is not a permanent cure. The injection "probably has to be repeated after several months." [21]

BrainStorm has collaborated with the University of Massachusetts, headed by Dr. Robert Brown, director of neurology, and with Dr. Merit Cudkowicz of Mass General Hospital, chief of neurology, to begin the BrainStorm trial in the United States.

The BrainStorm trial is designed to evaluate the safety and efficacy of transplantation of stem cells in 48 ALS patients. The cells will be administered via intramuscular and intrathecal injection. Patients will be followed monthly for three months before transplantation and for six months following. [22]

The trial is scheduled to commence in 2015, having received FDA approval for the trial in the United States. The trial will also be initiated later at the Mayo Clinic in Minnesota.
BrainStorm Cell Therapeutics Inc. announced [on October 20, 2014] that the FDA has designated NurOwn as a Fast Track product for the treatment of ALS. The FDA's Fast Track program is designed to expedite the review of drugs and biologics

---

21 http://www.hadassah.org/site/apps/nlnet/content2.aspx?c=keJNIWOvElH&b=7730783&ct=13928221
22 http://www.reuters.com/article/2014/04/28/us-brainstorm-fda-stemcells-id USKBN0DE0ZM20140428

intended to treat serious conditions and meet unmet medical needs through increased meetings and written communications with the FDA.[23] On January 5, 2015, Israel's BrainStorm Cell Therapeutics said final results from a clinical trial of its adult stem cell treatment in amyotrophic lateral sclerosis (ALS) were positive, with most patients showing a slowing in the disease's progression.

A single dose of the stem cell treatment called NurOwn was administered in a mid-stage phase 2a trial in 14 patients with ALS, at Hadassah Medical Center in Jerusalem.

"Nearly all subjects in this study experienced clinical benefit from treatment with NurOwn" the company said. . . .

Of the 12 patients with three or more months of follow-up, 92 percent experienced an improvement in disease progression. NurOwn slowed the progression of ALS using two different parameters and had a strong effect on the rate of decline in lung function, BrainStorm said.

"We observed not just a highly meaningful slowing of ALS progression on two different parameters . . . but subjects with prolonged stabilization and even improvements in function. And this was achieved with just a single dose of NurOwn," said BrainStorm Chief Executive Tony Fiorino.

BrainStorm, which is also conducting clinical trials at three sites in the United States, plans to move to a study in the next few months to see if the results can be amplified with repeated doses.[24]

Cedars-Sinai Stem-Cell Program

The Cedars-Sinai Regenerative Medicine Institute was awarded a $17.8 million grant from the California Institute for Regenerative Medicine to develop stem-cell treatments for patients with ALS.

---

23 http://www.als.net/Media/5470/News/

24 http://uk.reuters.com/article/2015/01/05/us-brainstorm-cell-als-idUKKBN 0KE0Z820150105

The grant . . . will fund a project with combined stem cell and gene therapy to treat [ALS] with stem cells found in early brain development and a protein called GDNF that promotes the survival of neurons [see Neuralstem section earlier]. The stem cells alone have the potential to protect damaged motor neurons in ALS. This potential increases when combined with the additional known effects of GDNF. In the past, delivering GDNF to the brain or spinal cord has been nearly impossible because it does not cross from the blood to the tissue of the spinal cord.

"We're looking at a novel and exciting way of using stem cells as 'Trojan horses' that arrive at the sick motor neurons and deliver the protein exactly where it's needed," [stated] Clive Svendsen, PhD, director of the Regenerative Medicine Institute and leader of the project. "Our early study indicates this approach has significant potential, and we're excited to bring this treatment a step closer to helping ALS patients." [25]

New Gene Therapy by Voyager

A Cambridge biotechnology company [launched in February 2014] is taking aim at Parkinson's disease and ALS with a new gene therapy that deliberately infects patients with a virus.

The firm, Voyager Therapeutics, plans to use a class of viruses known as adeno-associated viruses as carriers to deliver vital proteins to the brain. Intentional infection may be counterintuitive, but the viruses used in the therapy are harmless to humans, making them ideal vehicles for moving proteins through the body. . . . Boston venture capital firm Third

---

25 http://www.cedars-sinai.edu/About-Us/News/News-Releases-2012/Cedars-Sinai-Awarded-$178-Million-Grant-to-Develop-ALS-Treatment.aspx

Rock Ventures considered Voyager's research so promising that it invested $45 million to get the company off the ground, an unusually big bet on such an early-stage life sciences firm.

The investment reflects a broader belief among the scientific community that gene therapy could be the key to effectively treating some of the world's most challenging disorders. Gene therapy techniques typically involve replacing a mutated gene with a healthy version or turning off a gene that causes disease.

Voyager plans to use adeno-associated viruses as carriers for both techniques. To treat Parkinson's for instance, Voyager will use viruses to deliver a missing protein. For [ALS], the viruses will help shut down a harmful protein.

Expecting gene therapy to produce cures for rare diseases might be unrealistic [according to Mark Levin, Third Rock cofounder], "but the idea is to make a dramatic difference in patients' lives." [26]

THE U.S FOOD AND DRUG ADMINISTRATION (FDA)

When it comes to the fabled and powerful Food and Drug Administration (FDA), let me be blunt: it is too conservative; It is too slow to act; it lacks compassion; and it needs to change now to save lives! Change for the betterment of ALS patients is absolutely imperative!

The FDA definitely needs to restructure how it approves new drugs that have been proven safe and that can help even some people in a clinical trial, even if the drugs in question do not show efficacy for the majority of the people in a group. Since each person is a unique individual, the disease may also vary uniquely by individual. The FDA, without a doubt, should allow certain drugs—for example, R(+)Pramipexole, which is available and does help some people to be prescribed under certain conditions, such as when a drug might help an ALS patient. Otherwise, to obtain such a drug off label without a prescription is almost financially prohibitive for most families. Our daughter, with the help of her family and friends, is paying $37,500 per year for access to R(+)Pramipexole alone.

When people have a fatal illness, they ought to be able to take just about anything they believe can help, at a reasonable price, but that's unfortunately not the case today. And that needs to be dramatically changed!

The FDA was established to protect the public's interest, not to prevent them from getting help! Some of its rules and regulations are unquestionably outdated; in particular, they are too conservative with regard to R(+)Pramipexole, Generon, and other similar drugs and stem cell therapies. This is especially true for therapies that target rare or fatal diseases, such as ALS, where no other drugs or procedures are available to either save a life or, at the very least, to extend a life until something better comes along.

The FDA is too slow in approving drugs and procedures that have demonstrated both safety and efficacy in Phase I and Phase II human clinical trials, even if they did not meet the more stringent criteria in a Phase III trial, which tests new drugs on a larger scale. This is primarily relevant to fatal or rare diseases where there is no cure and the patients have no hope for survival. To reiterate, the FDA should allow those individuals who may or do benefit from a drug that has proven safe (even if they are in the minority) to have access to that drug instead of making it unavailable until it has proven both safe and efficacious, over a much longer period of time, for the majority participating in large trials (i.e. Phase III). Concomitantly, the manufacturer of such drugs should then compassionately make them available at reasonable cost to the ALS patients in need of them. This could be assured with a price control, regulated by the FDA and based on the cost of the drugs to be produced while allowing the manufacturer some degree of reasonable profit, and applied to only fatal or rare diseases. It is referred to as "accelerated distribution" while being tested further in Phase III.

Congress needs to act without delay to change some FDA policies in order to save lives—out of compassion for humanity. Legislation should be introduced in Congress to require the FDA to meet the needs of all citizens of our nation.

In late December 2013, the "Right to Try" bill started making its way through the Arizona state legislature. The basic premise of the bill is that patients with fatal and incurable diseases should be able to choose for themselves whether or not to try an experimental drug. The bill's authors state that they should not be constrained by the FDA's approval process. What also could constrain the patient is the exceedingly high manufacturer's cost, passed on in price to the consumer, of some of these experimental drugs. Of course, that drug could become even more expensive if it is ever approved.

A step ahead of Arizona is Colorado; it is the first state to actually enact "Right to Try" legislation, which is designed to give seriously ill patients access to novel, nonapproved therapies (and bypassing the FDA). Richard Garr, CEO of Neuralstem, stated after the legislation was passed, "This is something the entire industry will have to deal with. Patient access is becoming a really big issue in the U.S., with patients going to social media to demand they get treatments. This access is even more meaningful once the treatment has proven safe through clinical trials in Phase I and II. Such treatment may not prove efficacious to a majority, especially in Phase III, but it could very well show efficacy and be helpful to some of the patients. At least this gives them a fighting chance!" [27]

ORPHAN STATUS FOR ALS

The FDA has given "orphan status" to certain ALS drugs and other treatments associated with this rare disease. This protects the patent for this group of drugs and treatments so that once approved by the FDA for distribution, the companies producing

---

27 personal statement made to the author

these drugs and treatments have an exclusive right to market their products for a certain period of time before a competitive drug or treatment can enter the marketplace. Because there is such a large cost to developing drugs and treatments, this gives the producing company time to recoup their expenses and possibly also profit from their research efforts prior to other companies competing in the same market. Thus, for that purpose, orphan status is given to drugs/treatments where the total number of people affected is low (relatively speaking), so there is often not a chance to sell enough products to recoup cost and make a profit unless given this prolonged extra period of time without competition.

LACK OF FUNDS FOR ALS RESEARCH: A MAJOR PROBLEM

ALS is a horrific disease, yet there is a definite dearth of ALS research. Because ALS is such a rare disease that affects only 30,000 Americans, with just 5,000 new cases diagnosed each year, major drug companies are reluctant to utilize their research monies for finding a cure by a drug or other therapy because of the lack of potential for company profits. What is overlooked is the fact that, unfortunately, the average lifespan of those affected with ALS is only two to five years. While there are approximately 5,000 new cases each year, the reason only 30,000 cases remain annually is because approximately 5,000 patients also die of this terrible disease each year. Thus, patient numbers do not accumulate, and that 30,000 number of cases remains static; annual deaths preclude it from growing into a larger number that can be treated by new drugs and other therapies.

Major drug companies are cautious about investing their research dollars in finding a cure for ALS, or even, at the very least, to turn ALS into a chronic rather than a fatal disease. Therefore it is vital that, besides orphan status, major research funds come from elsewhere so patients can be treated profitably by new drugs and therapies.

ALS and Private Fund-Raising Activities

Because there is such a lack of research from the pharmaceutical community, individual efforts can and do help the cause. Since our daughter Marjie was diagnosed in September 2009, our family and friends alone have raised well over $100,000 to beat Lou Gehrig's disease.

Within two months, our grandson Spencer Silver (who was twelve years old at that time), son of Marjie's sister Debbie, held a two-weekend estate/garage sale, which he called "Miracle for Marjie," in Boca Raton, Florida. Over 100 families donated items and time to help at the sale. A local businessman donated the warehouse space to hold the sale. A local moving company donated movers and a truck to deliver the items that people donated and purchased. Items were set up like a department store in different rooms of the building, including electronics and everyday items ranging from computers to stereos to TVs, indoor and outdoor furniture, clothing, baby/nursery toys, bed/bath items, art work, and more.

Spencer was like a carnival barker on the microphone, announcing special sales in the different departments. To encourage buyers, he would set up specials such as "Two for the price of one" or "Everything on this table only $1.00 for the next three minutes," creating energy and excitement among the buyers to help the items sell out. He and his friends dressed up in costumes (that also were being sold) holding up signs for cars to stop and come to the sales event. Over $25,000 was raised in two weekends, and 100 percent of funds raised were donated to the ALS Association.

While Madison Silver, younger sister of Spencer, was helping at the garage sale, she, too, was figuring out what she personally could do to make a difference. She began to create watercolor paintings of the word "Hope" in all different designs, incorporating them into her stationery. In each painting there can be found her own "silver heart" design. Just months after the garage sale success, Madison created a website called HopeheART by Madison, and for a donation for a cure, she sent donors a gift of her stationery made with "hope straight from her heart." This project raised over $53,000, and again, 100 percent of the hopeheART donations go to different ALS organizations that are at the cutting edge of science in finding a cure for ALS. (All stationery and shipping costs are donated by Madison Silver's family.)

Megan Spector (who was twelve years old at that time), daughter of Marjie's other sister, Sheri, used her own ingenuity and special talents to create another highly successful fund-raiser for a cure. Megan organized a benefit concert and silent auction in San Diego, California, called "Striking A Chord: A Benefit Concert to Help Beat ALS." Megan, with the help of other well-known performers in California, local merchants, and over 400 concert attendees in the Qualcomm Hall (offered by that company), raised over $35,000, with 100 percent of the proceeds going to ALS research and support. Megan also sang the national anthem at other ALS fund-raisers, including the Walk for ALS and the first and second annual University of San Diego ALS Basketball Men's Classics.

Marjie's sister Deborah Silver is a jazz/cabaret artist and makes CDs to sell with 100 percent of sales going to the same ALS cause. She has also performed benefit concerts to help raise money for an ALS cure.

Since Marjie's diagnosis, the family has vowed not to give gifts to one another for special occasions, only to continue to donate to help keep Marjie alive.

Marjie's close friends have staged two "Comic Hours" at the Comedy House in Hermosa Beach, California, to raise funds to help Marjie's medical expenses. They collected over $17,000 on those occasions. What true friends they all are.

Marjie herself is writing a caregiver's guide for the disabled from a patient's viewpoint. She looks forward to having this distributed to help all patients better communicate with their families and caregivers.

Even more recently, on Sunday, January 25, 2015, Spencer, age seventeen, staged a "Battle of the Bands" at Jazziz in Mizner Park with ten local South Florida bands competing and five celebrity judges. This charity event raised approximately $15,000 for ALS research.

As important as these and other individual and community fund-raising activities have been and continue to be, they are not nearly enough to stem the tide of this horrible disease. It's going to take so very much more!

THE CHALLENGE

This book presents a unique, bold, simplistic, and feasible plan to raise **a Billion dollars** for research to solve the ALS conundrum and BEAT ALS NOW! In order to effectuate the plan, it will take a major ALS organization (or other key organization) to step up and accept the responsibility of providing unrelenting determination and leadership until the goal has been achieved. The following three major ALS organizations offer the best possibilities of leading that crusade.

THE ALS ASSOCIATION

Established in 1985, the ALS Association is the only nonprofit organization fighting Lou Gehrig's disease on every front. By promoting global research, providing assistance for people with ALS through a nationwide network of chapters, coordinating multidisciplinary care through certified clinical care centers, and fostering government partnerships, the Association builds hope and enhances quality of life while searching for new treatments and a cure.

As a multifaceted ALS organization, the Association leads the way in combining research, care services, public education, and public policy—giving help and hope to those facing the disease. The Association's nationwide network of chapters provides comprehensive patient services and support to the ALS community. The stated mission of the ALS Association is to lead the fight to treat and cure ALS through global research and nationwide advocacy while also empowering people with Lou Gehrig's disease and their families to live fuller lives by providing them with compassionate care and support.

Its new national president and CEO is Barbara Newhouse, who recently replaced retiring Jane Gilbert. The ALS Association has thirty-eight chapters throughout the United States.

The ALS Association raises monies for ALS research, in addition to increasing public awareness, lobbying Congress for more support, and caring for ALS patients in ALS clinics around the country.

PROJECT A.L.S.

Jenifer Estess, born in 1963, was a theatrical producer and was diagnosed with ALS in 1997. After her diagnosis, she bravely, along with family and friends, formed Project A.L.S. "to defeat ALS and find a cure." She raised more than $17 million for that purpose and brought together scientists from different laboratories to cooperate in the search for a cure. That foundation, which has paid for investigations into genetics, stem cells, gene therapy, and accelerated drug testing, continues their multifaceted efforts today.

In 2001, Ms. Estess produced a movie for CBS television called *Jenifer* that told her own story. She also wrote her memoir,

Tales From the Bed: On Living, Dying and Having It All. In 2003, she died at the age of forty.

The goal of Project A.L.S. research is to discover the first effective treatments and a cure for ALS. The Project A.L.S. Research Advisory Board has identified and prioritized five strategies for 2013-2015 that hopefully will move the medical world closer to that goal. They refer to it as "5 IN 3"—five projects in three years—which range from basic research to preclinical studies.

Project A.L.S. is a non-profit, 501c3 organization. It professes to have raised over $55 million and has given 83 percent directly to ALS research. Jenifer's two sisters continue to lead Project A.L.S. Its president is Meredith Estess, and its director of research is Valerie Estess.

Project A.L.S. has the strong support of Hollywood and television celebrities. Among them are television's Jimmy Kimmel, Katie Couric, and Julianna Margulies (The Good Wife); and Hollywood's George Clooney, Ben Stiller, Andy Garcia, and Michael J. Fox, among a number of others. Additionally one of Hollywood's leading public relations firms, Baker/Winokur/Ryder, is another strong supporter of Project A.L.S. One of the firm's owners, Nanci Ryder, unfortunately has ALS. These contacts could be of immeasurable assistance in achieving goodwill and the support from the NFL and MLB.

TEAM GLEASON

My good friend Abe Tahir, a longtime resident of New Orleans and former owner of Tahir's Art Galleries in New Orleans, Houston, and Beverly Hills, knows of the plight of our daughter Marjie Block. He sent me an article from *Gambit*, a weekly publication of the BestofNewOrleans.com. It was written by Alex Woodward and published in January, 2014. Below are excerpts from that article:

No White Flags

Former New Orleans Saint Steve Gleason fights ALS and inspires the world by refusing to bow to a debilitating illness.

In 2012 the New Orleans Saints unveiled a bronze statue titled *Rebirth*—immortalizing former Saint Steve Gleason's 2006 punt block heard around the world. That blocked punt was in the opening minutes of the Saints first home game inside the Superdome following Hurricane Katrina. Gleason's play ignited a legendary Saints victory and quickly came to symbolize the region's grit and determination after Katrina.

Fast forward seven years from that game, and the once wild-haired burly Gleason is restricted to a wheelchair and communicates with the aid of a computer. He has been diagnosed with amyotrophic lateral sclerosis (ALS, also known as Lou Gehrig's disease), a debilitating illness that atrophies muscles and inhibits voluntary movement. In 2011, Gleason revealed his diagnosis. That same year Steve and Michel [his wife] gave birth to their son Rivers.

Tapping a seemingly bottomless well of strength and courage, he founded the Team Gleason organization to raise awareness of the disease and advocate for a cure. Among other achievements, the nonprofit announced plans last summer to build the Team Gleason House for Innovative Living at St. Margaret's Skilled Nursing Residence. The residential facility will help people diagnosed with incurable neuromuscular disorders live more independently.

Also last year, he wrote an in-depth essay for Sports Illustrated—using his eyes. An eye-tracking computer helps him type. Gleason's motto is "no white flags," and his message of perseverance not only has inspired people diagnosed with ALS worldwide but it also has become a message of hope to all who face struggles. Gleason wrote:

"Although we feel good about what we have accomplished, in terms of raising the level of awareness, there is more work to be done.

"Since Lou Gehrig's death, there have been no effective medical therapy developments for people with ALS.

"The newest science now and on the horizon is simply cost prohibitive unless produced on a large scale . . . If the ALS research market was flooded with funds and accountability, I think we would see much more unity and faster results."

(Reprinted with the kind permission of Alex Woodward, *Best of New Orleans*. Copyright 2014. *Gambit*.)

ALS VIDEO: NFL PLAYERS AND COACHES

A video was created for Steve Gleason's football family— by players and coaches of the NFL—to show that, whether they had lined up with him or against him on the field of play, they all supported him in his fight against this cruel and unrelenting disease.[28]

These outstanding players and coaches all stand by Steve's belief that everyone who gets diagnosed with this disease has the right to fight, has the right to proper treatment and to the best available care. And they believe, like Steve does, that ALS is underfunded, under-resourced and largely ignored. And that this is not okay.

The video represents the players' commitment to do something about that, including:

---

28 Woodward, A. January 7, 2014. "'No white flags': Steve Gleason, New Orleanian of the Year 2013." *Gambit*. BestofNewOrleans.com.

- Taking ALS out of the shadows and getting people talking about it.
- Getting the best and brightest scientific minds together and asking them what they need to cure ALS.
- Making some noise, pressuring the right people, and raising the money to make it all happen.

The video is a message from these elite players and coaches (listed below)—among the best and strongest in the world—to all the victims of this horrific disease to say: "We're all in this together. And it's an invitation to the rest of the world to join the fight and put all of our heads together to find a cure for ALS."

Below is a list of names of NFL players and coaches (from various teams in the NFL) participating in the video, which can be viewed on NFL Players & Coaches Stand Together to Cure ALS on YouTube.

Players and Coaches Speaking

Players: Steve Gleason, Drew Brees, Jonathan Vilma, Ray Lewis, Brendon Ayanbadejo, Thomas Morstead, Bill Romanowski, Jeff Saturday, Ronnie Lott, Joe Flacco, Lance Moore, Clay Matthews, Scott Fujita, Steven Jackson, Aaron Rodgers, Trent Dilfer, Charles Woodson.

Coaches: Mike McCarthy, Dick Vermeil, Herman Edwards

NFL Players Association (NFLPA): Jason Belser and DeMaurice Smith

Other Nonspeaking Players in the Video: Jed Collins, Mark Ingram, Brian de la Puente, Ryan Nece, Chris Kluwe, Antonio Pierce, Eric Barton, Zach Strief, D'Qwell Jackson, O. J. Brigance,

Eric Barton, Cornelius Bennett, Kevin Mawae, Akbar Gbaja-Biamila, Trent Edwards, Brian Waters, Ben Watson, Alex Mack, Joe Thomas, Phil Dawson, Ray Ventrone, Curtis DeLoatch, Jon Stinchcomb.

Steve Gleason's efforts and this strong public support from forty NFL players, three NFL coaches, and two NFLPA reps represents a major base from which to launch a strategic campaign through the National Football League to cure ALS!

OTHER MAJOR ALS ORGANIZATIONS

ALS WORLDWIDE

ALS Worldwide is a nonprofit organization dedicated to the support of ALS patients and families. Its efforts focus on obtaining and providing information, advice, direction, support, guidance, hope, and research.

Stephen and Barbara Byer, founders and co-executive directors of ALS Worldwide, tragically lost a son, Ben, to this dreadful disease in 2008. For six years prior to his death, they worked diligently and unsuccessfully to find an effective treatment to save his life. They continue to be as dedicated as anyone has ever been to helping find a cure.

The Byers have collaborated with Dr. James P. Bennett, who discovered R(+)Pramipexole. With FDA approval, they have a small number of patients they are following that continue to receive that drug through them.

They are also part of a recently formed "Research Consortium," investigating a new ALS drug that they feel could have great potential. The drug is named MicroNeurotrophin.

Quarterly, they publish and distribute an updated newsletter on the progress of ongoing ALS research projects and on the latest new ones in the "pipeline."

Recently the Byers published the "Best Standards of Practice for ALS Clinics and Hospitals." It is the culmination of their review of ALS clinics and hospitals throughout the world and their interviews with patients, physicians, hospitals, and clinics.

THE NORTHEAST ALS CONSORTIUM

The Northeast ALS Consortium (NEALS) is an international, independent, nonprofit group of researchers who collaboratively conduct clinical research on amyotrophic lateral sclerosis (ALS) and other motor neuron diseases. Their mission is to translate scientific advances into new treatments for people with ALS and motor neuron disease as rapidly as possible.

This consortium is a group that works together as well as with scientists, patients, and family members in 100 sites in the US and Canada to conduct clinical research together and bring therapies to patients close to their homes. They have trained these centers in ALS outcome measures; they work with a group of scientists to identify the top candidates to bring forward to trials; and they have set up processes to do this quickly.

Their expertly trained research sites, investigators, and management staff help to relieve the burden of running a clinical trial. Their expertise can reduce the amount of time and money spent on clinical research so they can find a cure faster.[29]

The NEALS network has over fifteen years of experience in developing and conducting multi-center clinical trials in ALS and motor neuron disease. NEALS can help sponsors interested in developing new studies design protocol, select sites, and manage trials.[30]

Tara Lincoln is the current NEALS program director, and Dr. Merit Cudkowicz is the current co-chairperson.

29 http://www.alsconsortium.org/about_us.php
30 http://www.alsconsortium.org/neals_cro_capabilities.php

ADDITIONAL ALS RESEARCH ORGANIZATIONS

Besides the ALS Association, Project A.L.S., Team Gleason, and the other major ALS research organizations, together with their current trials as noted earlier, there are a number of other leading ALS research organizations and doctors. Some of the most active and prominent are:

- ALS Therapy Alliance; Dr. Robert Brown and associates
- University of Massachusetts; Dr. Robert Brown, Chair and Professor of Neurology
- ALS Therapy Development Institute; Dr. Steve Perrin, Director
- Massachusetts General; Dr. Merit Cudkowicz, ALS Clinic, Chief of Neurology, Massachusetts General; Professor of Neurology, Harvard Medical School
- University of California, San Diego; Dr. Donald W. Cleveland, ALS Principal Investigator
- Howard Hughes Medical Center, San Diego; Dr. Larry Goldstein
- University of California, San Diego; Dr. John M. Ravits, Head, ALS Translation Research
- Director, Dr. Richard Smith, San Diego, The Scripps Institute
- Virginia Commonwealth University, Department of Neurology; Dr. James P. Bennett Jr., Bemiss Professor
- State University of New York, Upstate Medical University; Dr. Jeremy Shefner
- Harvard Stem Cell Institute; Dr. Kevin C. Eggan, researcher
- Neuromuscular Program and ALS Center, Penn State College Of Medicine and Penn State Hershey Medical Center; Dr. Zachary Simmons
- Mayo Clinic
- University Of California, Irvine, Dr. Tahseen Mozaffar
- The Forbes Norris MDA/ALS Research and Treatment Center, San Francisco, Dr. Robert G. Miller, Director

- Houston Methodist Hospital System, Stanley H. Appel, MD
- Gladstone Institute University of California, San Francisco, Steve Finkbeiner, MD, PhD
- Northwestern University Feinberg School of Medicine

ALS AND THE NFL

In early 2013 my wife, Sondy, and I recommended to the ALS Association and its president, Jane Gilbert, that they approach the NFL and implore them to become involved in helping to find a cure for ALS, using the Steve Gleason story and the video of the NFL players and coaches as a springboard to precipitate their interest and further involvement.

Shortly afterward, on February 22, 2013, we participated in a telephonic ALS Association "NFL Strategy Meeting" for that purpose. Afterward we presented a written suggested plan of action for approaching NFL Commissioner Roger Goodell for his support. While the committee as a whole felt the plan had merit, some members believed the matter would be too sensitive to the commissioner, since at least fourteen NFL players and former players have been diagnosed with ALS, including Steve Gleason, O.J. Brigance, and Kevin Turner, among others. Since there is a strong possibility that some cases of ALS may have been caused by blows to the head, the NFL would not want to be blamed. However, due to the advent of the phenomenal "Ice Bucket Challenge" as described later in this chapter, which has brought both vast new awareness of ALS and sizable new donations for ALS research, and the fact that Roger Goodell himself actively participated in an Ice Bucket Challenge, dedicating it to Steve Gleason, he may actually lend his support to my latest plan for NFL participation.

Nevertheless, there is an even more realistic, and much stronger, approach to getting the NFL involved in helping to find a cure for ALS. After due consideration, perhaps it's best when introducing this important endeavor to Commissioner Roger Goodell to simultaneously work through and get the support of the NFL Players Association and its members—who are directly affected! Based on the number of retired NFL players with ALS, medical reports have stated that because of brain injuries, NFL players are eight times more likely to be diagnosed with ALS than the average adult male, and military personnel are two times more likely to be diagnosed with ALS.[31] Those are meaningful statistics. Without the players, there would be no NFL.

With the groundwork already begun by leading NFL players and coaches in the video described earlier, the National Football League, representing the nation's most popular sport, could be an immense weapon in raising both awareness and funds to help defeat ALS.

Latest figures show 17,282,225 people annually attend this biggest live spectator sport in the world. By adding only $1 to the price of every NFL ticket sold annually, matched by an equal figure from NFL Management, we could raise $34,564,450 each year in the fight against ALS.

We also could enlist the additional fund-raising support of NFL corporate sponsors such as Papa John's, FedEx, Marriott, Verizon, GM, Visa, and Gatorade/Pepsi.

Why ALS and the NFL? Because that cruel fatal disease, with no cure, has the potential of directly affecting every player in the NFL far more than the general public. Because such an effort would support those NFL players who have been diagnosed with ALS or may be in the future. Because little public recognition is given to the relationship between ALS and football head injuries. Because there is a huge deficit in funding for ALS research. And because one of the greatest sporting figures of all times, New York Yankee Lou Gehrig (a teammate of Babe Ruth), died from ALS in the prime of his baseball career.

---

31 http://www.bumc.bu.edu/busm/2010/08/17/researchers-discover-brain-trauma-in-sports

ALS AND MAJOR LEAGUE BASEBALL

Why ALS and the MLB? Remembering Lou Gehrig brings us to the point that Major League Baseball, of all sports, should follow the fund-raising path suggested for the NFL earlier, designating a portion of ticket sales (matched by donations from ownership and management) to ALS research. Additionally, they could designate some of their games throughout the season and/ or the World Series to a Beat Lou Gehrig's Disease campaign. It's been almost seventy-five years since Lou Gehrig's famous "Luckiest Man on the Face of the Earth" speech at Yankee Stadium; it's more than time to do something about ALS!

Latest statistics reveal that over the long baseball season, 74,026,895 fans attend Major League Baseball games annually.[32] Adding only $1 to the price of every MLB ticket sold annually could raise $74,026,895 for ALS. Matching donations by MLB ownership and management would raise the huge amount of $148,053,790 annually in the fight to eradicate ALS. New Commissioner Rob Manfred should be contacted with this recommendation at the same time that the NFL Players Association is asked for their support.

Major League Baseball has already begun to take the lead in raising awareness of ALS by joining with leading ALS organizations in recognition of the 75th Anniversary of Lou Gehrig's speech during the year 2014. Together they introduced a new commemorative logo patch to honor those affected by that destructive disease.

On July 2, 2014, at the New York Yankees home game, the team hosted annual recognition festivities, with additional promotions around the 75th Anniversary. All players wore the commemorative logo patch.

On July 4, 2014, all players, managers, coaches, and umpires wore a special uniform logo patch. All home clubs also

---

32 http://mlb.mlb.com/news/article.jsp?ymd=20131001&content_id=6228
    2120&vkey=pr_mlb&c_id=mlb

hosted pregame ceremonies recognizing those affected by the disease, and paid tribute to all who are leading efforts to raise awareness and to support finding a cure.

The 75th anniversary of Lou Gehrig's death on June 2, 1941, will be in 2016 during a major political event—the presidential campaign and election—and during baseball season, followed by football season. What a great victory for humankind if, on or even before that period of time, major progress can be made to prevent and even cure ALS!

BEAT THE CLOCK—BEAT ALS NOW!

For those stricken with ALS, time is definitely of the essence!

By taking the approach described earlier—adding only $1.00 to the price of every NFL and MLB ticket sold annually, matched by donations from NFL and MLB ownership and management—a total of $182,618,240 could be raised annually for ALS Research! This huge amount, combined with what is raised annually by Augie's Quest (see below), and CVS's annual ALS drive, could bring in nearly $200 million each year to beat ALS!

If NFL and MLB owners are skeptical about raising the price of their tickets by a mere $1.00, and question if it would dampen the enthusiasm or reduce the number of attendees each year (as unlikely as that would be), then in the name of humanity, they should fund the money themselves, especially since this charitable donation would be tax deductible for their organizations.

With a five-year plan in place, such a historic effort could raise approximately one billion dollars for ALS research! And there's hope that ALS could be cured before all of those dollars are expended.

Admittedly, this is a bold and brash approach. However, the sporting world is where the money is, and both the NFL and MLB definitely have their reasons to attack and help find a cure for ALS/Lou Gehrig's disease. After the plan is fully considered, if there remain questions about this particular plan, then the NFL and MLB should devise plans of their own, encouraged and supported by all ALS organizations. Just talking about the disease and the need for awareness will not get the job done! That's like "spitting in the ocean, waiting on high tide"!

Once the NFL and MLB join together and combine to "throw" such a massive amount of funds toward ALS research, progress toward a cure should be expedited, and large pharmaceutical companies would be more inclined to join the fight to cure this fatal disease. Together we will score a major victory for humankind and knock out ALS for good! What a blessing that would be to 30,000 Americans living with ALS, and the 5,000 more diagnosed each year, plus all the others afflicted with ALS around the world.

AUGIE'S QUEST: JOIN THE NFL AND THE MLB IN A BIGGER QUEST!

Augustine (Augie) Nieto, a prominent leader in the nation's fitness industry for nearly three decades, received a diagnosis of ALS in March 2005. Augie, fifty-five, is considered a pioneer in the health fitness industry. He is cofounder and former president of Life Fitness, which produces and distributes Life Fitness exercise products to multiple health centers and gyms throughout the country. In 2005 he received the fitness industry's top honor, the Lifetime Achievement award.

Augie Nieto is chairman of the ALS Therapy Development Institute (ALS TDI).

Frustrated with the progress of ALS research in particular, Augie combined his entrepreneurial skills and determination, along with the help of his supportive wife, Lynne, to found Augie's Quest in order to raise funds to increase and expedite ALS research. Since its formation, Augie's Quest has raised more than $44 million for research with the ALS Therapy Development Institute (ALS TDI), which continues its preclinical efforts to find a drug with enough promise and financial backing to bring to an ALS human clinical trial. It is currently clinically testing the drug Gilenya, which is already on the market for multiple sclerosis.

Augie's Quest has demonstrated Augie Nieto's extraordinary efforts in seeking a cure for ALS.

With Augie's fine reputation in the fitness industry, he surely is widely recognized, highly respected, and has important contacts with numerous leading colleges and national sports figures. Because of his unparalleled efforts, he should unquestionably be one of the first to be asked to join this ALS special crusade, with the NFL and MLB to cure Lou Gehrig's disease!

CURT SHILLING, MAJOR LEAGUE BASEBALL, AND ALS

Curt Schilling, former six-time all-star major league baseball pitcher for the Boston Red Sox, and ESPN analyst for *Sunday Night Baseball* has been a longtime proponent for eradicating ALS.

According to an Internet article by Gary Wosk on the ALS Association's website,

> [In 2009,] the ALS Association inducted . . . Curt Schilling and his wife Shonda into the organization's Hall of Fame as its first inductees for their long time support of The Association in the fight against Lou Gehrig's disease. . . . The Schillings were recognized by the Association for their sustained and dedicated efforts in advocacy, awareness, and fund-raising, for significantly

impacting research and patient care programs provided by The Association to find a cause and cure for ALS, and to improve quality of life for people living with the disease, their families and caregivers.

"Curt and Shonda Schilling have devoted virtually nonstop effort in support of The ALS Association's vital programs and services that have enriched the quality of life for people living with ALS," said Jane H. Gilbert, president and CEO of The Association.

The Schillings, who have raised more than $10 million for The Association through their "Curt's Pitch for ALS," "Covering All the Bases," "Say It with Flowers," and numerous other fund-raisers, remain steadfast in their dedication to curing ALS.[33]

While pitching for the Red Sox in the 2004 American League Championship Series (ALCS), Schilling wrote "KALS" on his right shoe for the entire world television audience to see. The "K" stands for strike out. In that series, down three games to zero, the Red Sox overcame insurmountable odds to defeat the New York Yankees to become ALCS champs and go on to win the World Series. When Curt Schilling pitched in game six of the ALCS series, close to a billion people worldwide watched as his ankle bled, but more importantly, they saw the phrase "KALS" written on his shoe. The Schillings even have a son named Gehrig.

Unfortunately, Curt has been diagnosed with cancer of the mouth, which is currently in remission. He also had a heart attack in 2011, after which a stent was placed in one of his arteries. Curt said, "I've always believed life is about embracing the gifts and rising up to meet the challenges. . . . My father left me with a saying that I've carried my entire life: 'Tough times don't last, tough people do.'"[34]

---

33 http://web.alsa.org/site/PageServer?pagename=NewsArchive_051209_A
34 http://espn.go.com/mlb/story/_/id/10403896/curt-schilling-diagnosed-cancer

I am confident Curt Schilling and his wife, Shonda, who has also had health problems, will, if possible, join in this new, huge effort to get MLB and its commissioner Rob Manfred to combine with the NFL, under the auspices of a major ALS organization, to "Strike Out ALS" once and for all.

TOMMY LASORDA, MAJOR LEAGUE BASEBALL, AND ALS

Some years ago, while president of the Rotary Club of Jackson, I met the great baseball legend Tommy Lasorda at a Rotary function in Los Angeles. I asked him if he would be kind enough to come to Jackson, Mississippi, and speak to our 350-member Rotary Club. He didn't hesitate to accept my invitation. He just said, "Send me a plane ticket, and I will be there." Former Mississippi Lt. Governor Brad Dye and his family were personal friends of Tommy and attended. I invited their son to have the privilege of introducing our esteemed speaker. Beforehand I told one of my favorite stories to describe Tommy Lasorda. It is entitled "The Oyster and the Eagle," which I heard many years ago.

The Oyster and the Eagle

When God made the oyster, he gave it a shell to protect it, where it lies at the bottom of the ocean. When it is hungry, all it needs to do is to open its shell and food rushes in. But when God made the eagle, He said, "'Go and build yourself a home." And the eagle built it on the mountaintop, where storms threaten it every day. For food it flies thorough miles of rain, wind, sleet, and snow. It is unafraid of danger or risk. The eagle, not the oyster, is the symbol or our great country.

And I concluded, "Tommy Lasorda is one of the great eagles of the sporting world!"

I am confident that once the plan is in motion, Tommy Lasorda will lend his famous name in the fight to beat ALS (Lou Gehrig's disease) and support Commissioner Rob Manfred and Major League Baseball's effort in that regard.

His speech to the Rotary Club of Jackson was one of the most hilarious, inspirational, and best talks ever made before the large crowd of members and guests who attended.

Combining the NFL, MLB, and Augie's Quest, under the auspices of a major ALS organization in the "Crusade to Strikeout ALS" would be the largest effort ever made to accomplish that goal since Lou Gehrig's passing almost seventy-five years ago. In the military, when a target needs to be destroyed, all firepower available is coordinated and concentrated on it until it is obliterated. That is exactly what needs to be done to ALS!

The ALS Ice Bucket Challenge

A perfect example of the concentration of "Fire Power" can be found in the ALS Ice Bucket Challenge, which began in July of 2014 to raise awareness of ALS and raise funds for research. According to *NBC News,*

> The challenge started in Massachusetts with former Boston College baseball player Pete Frates, who was diagnosed with the disease in 2012. . . . Frates, who can no longer speak, posted his own ice bucket video to the tune of Vanilla Ice's "Ice, Ice Baby" and dared a few people to try it. A social media firestorm ensued, extending well beyond the gates of Boston College.
>
> After posting their ice bucket videos to social media, participants nominate others to take the plunge

and keep the cycle going. If those challenged don't accept within 24 hours, they're asked to donate to ALS research or to the charity of their choice.

Many accepted the challenge and donated significant funds! I first heard about the challenge from our daughter Sheri Spector of San Diego. Since then, all our children and grandchildren have taken the "challenge."

The *NBC News* report continues,

Challenge accepted or not, donations have been pouring in. According to the ALS Association spokeswoman, Carrie Munk, the organization has collected (at the time of her report) $1.35 million from July 29 to August 11. That's not counting donations to chapter offices around the country, Munk said. During the same time period last year, donations totaled $22,000.

"The monetary contributions are amazing, but there is so much value to the visibility that this is generating" Munk said. "It's unquantifiable"!

Pete Frates' parents, Nancy and John, joined more than 200 Bostonians who took the Ice Bucket Challenge, in Copley Square, challenging New York City, Los Angeles and Chicago to do the same.

According to the ALS Association, 50 percent of the American public doesn't know what the disease is. But as Frates' story has spread, the Ice Bucket challenge has become a call to arms for his family and friends to raise money and awareness for the disease, for which there is no cure.

"Who knew all it would take was a bag of ice and a bucket?" John Frates said. [35]

---

35   http://www.nbcnews.com/feature/making-a-difference/striking-out-als-ice-bucket-challenge-brings-flood-donations-n177896

So who among the notables have taken the Ice Bucket Challenge thus far? Ethel Kennedy and her family at Hyannis Port, Massachusetts; she challenged President Obama. Others are Matt Lauer, Martha Stewart, Boston Mayor Marty Walsh, New England Patriots wide receiver Julian Edelman, who challenged Patriot teammates Rob Gronkowski and Tom Brady. Others have been President George W. Bush and his wife, Laura; Bill Gates, Mark Zukenburg, Oprah Winfrey, and many other famous people, too many to name here.

Also, as mentioned earlier, none other than Roger Goodell, NFL Commissioner, stepped up for the Ice Bucket Challenge, which he dedicated to former New Orleans Saints safety Steve Gleason, who, as stated earlier in this book, has ALS. On his video, Goodell stated, "Hello everyone, I'm Roger Goodell. I want to thank (ex-NFL linebacker) Scott Fujita for nominating me for the ALS ice bucket challenge. I'm honored to accept the challenge and make a donation on behalf of Team Gleason. When I dry off from this, I'm going to challenge [Seattle Seahawks coach] Pete Carroll, and Michael Strahan [former New York Giants defensive end and new member of the NFL Hall of Fame.]"[36]

NHL free agent Paul "Biznasty" Bissonnette upped the stakes by having glacier water dropped on his head from a helicopter on top of a mountain.

Approaching the final edit of this book and according to the *Washington Business Journal,* over $200 million has been donated through the Ice Bucket Challenge from around the globe.[37] What a boost this Ice Bucket Challenge has given to ALS awareness and research funding, in addition to the Billion Dollar Challenge I have made to a major ALS organization, the NFL, MLB, and Augie's Quest in this book.

---

36 http://ftw.usatoday.com/2014/08/roger-goodell-ice-bucket-challenge

37 http://www.bizjournals.com/washington/news/2014/12/12/ice-bucket-challenge-has-raised-220-million.html

22

USING VITAL ALS RESEARCH FUNDS— A RAINBOW ON THE HORIZON

Due to the conundrum around what causes ALS, the way ALS attacks the body in multiple ways, and the harshness of its effects on the body, it will likely take more than one drug or one therapeutic method to slow the way ALS progresses relentlessly, and more than one way to effect a cure—just as surgery, radiation, chemotherapy, and drugs are all combined to fight cancer. The scientific and medical community, therefore, needs to consider a multifaceted approach—combining pharmaceutical drugs, stem-cells therapies, and possibly genetic therapy—to ultimately defeat this cruel and powerful disease.

To accomplish this, it would be most advantageous for ALS research to be coordinated under *one central umbrella organization.*

The major ALS organization that accepts the lead in this crusade to BEAT ALS NOW should form an entirely separate research division, under its auspices, to be the umbrella organization that coordinates research and allocates the new funds raised through this special and particular crusade. This umbrella organization should have its own president and board of directors, including members from the NFL and MLB, NFL and MLB Players Associations, the National ALS Association,

Project A.L.S., Team Gleason, ALS Worldwide, Northeast ALS Consortium, Augie's Quest, ALS Therapy Alliance, and the National Institutes of Health. This would comprise a very strong coalition to defeat ALS. It should also have its own corporate attorney and CPA firm for its annual report. Every single dollar raised in this new crusade must be allocated to ALS research and only to ALS research. Not one dollar from it should be spent on administration or for any other purpose. Such administration should be completely handled by the lead ALS organization and have no strings attached. The cost of administration needs to be fully defrayed by the parent lead organization itself. Additionally, annual allocations and any results achieved should be made transparent and published in an audited public report each year.

It is imperative to note here and must be emphasized that each separate ALS research project and organization will *continue to maintain its own autonomy and ability to raise ALS research funds for its own research efforts.* Any new funds allocated to it by the new umbrella organization will be in addition to the dollars autonomous groups raise through their own efforts.

Furthermore, the new umbrella organization, set up as a separate division under auspices of the lead ALS organization for this new crusade does not include, nor is it setup to receive or interfere with donations from any individuals, private organizations, foundations, corporations, or governmental agencies that normally contribute for ALS research, or to other ALS organizations of any kind. Its income is to be generated solely from the NFL and MLB.

But where and to whom should these new massive, mobilized funds be granted?

The normal method of spreading paltry research funds by selecting researchers who appear to have the possibility of solving a part of the ALS conundrum will not be enough to find the solutions needed to save thousands of lives in the near future—those 30,000 ALS victims of today plus the 5,000 new cases each year over the next several years. Development of potential therapies to treat rare diseases and ultra-rare diseases like ALS has mostly been the province of small university labs and a few small biotech companies. Recently, this has changed to a degree, but not nearly enough. A much better approach needs to be made, with a considerably stronger sense of urgency!

The Ice Bucket Challenge, which raised over $200 million intended for ALS research, has begun to drastically change that, providing a much greater opportunity for ALS research to expeditiously find a cure. Most everyone donating to the Ice Bucket Challenge expected to have their funds applied directly to ALS research, since that is the *only way to find a cure*. However, according to a direct conversation this author had in May 2015 with two ALSA representatives at their Washington headquarters, at the present time, the ALS Association intends to apply 68 percent of the $115 million donated funds it received to research. It is only assumed from that statement that the remainder will be utilized for support of their thirty-eight ALS clinics, lobbying, awareness, and administration. My Billion Dollar Plan applies 100 percent of the funds to research and research alone!

This major *one-time* infusion of funds into the ALS Association is unprecedented since Lou Gehrig died from the disease almost seventy-five years ago. To promptly implement these funds to find a cure for ALS, the ALS Association Research Institute has allocated the first $22.6 million to begin four major initiatives. They are:

INITIATIVE 1: ALS Accelerated Therapeutics (ALS ACT).[38]

In partnership with General Electric, a leading global research and technology company, and the Neurological Clinical Research Institute at Massachusetts General Hospital (MGH), ALS ACT will enact a multipronged approach to expediting clinical trials in ALS.

---

38 Initiatives 1-4 taken directly *Research ALS Today,* Volume 15, Fall 2014.

INITIATIVE 2: CONSORTIUM FOR GENOMICS OF NEURODEGENERATIVE DISEASE

The purpose of this initiative is to harness state-of-the-art genetic, genomic, and bioinformatics tools to gain insights into motor neuron disease mechanisms and to use this knowledge to identify new diagnostic and therapeutic approaches.

INITIATIVE 3: NEUROCOLLABORATIVE

This initiative will employ a three-pronged approach drawing on the unparalleled expertise of the three associated labs. Donald Cleveland, PhD, of the University of California, San Diego, will spearhead the development of antisense therapy against the C9orf72 gene, the most common genetic cause of ALS; Steven Finkbeiner, MD, PhD, of the Gladstone Institutes at the University of California, San Francisco, will further develop robotic technology for screening drugs in motor neuron cell culture; targets include reducing protein misfolding and increasing misfolded protein clearance mechanisms, both key problems in ALS; and Clive Svendsen, PhD, of Cedars-Sinai Medical Center in Los Angeles, who will develop the Stem Cell and Motor Neuron Core Facility to create clinical-grade induced pluripotent stem (iPS) cell lines, which will be openly shared with the ALS research community. iPS cells have emerged as a key research tool and potential source of therapeutic cells in ALS, and iPS cells are a key source of motor neurons for drug discovery efforts, such as those at the Gladstone Center.[39]

INITIATIVE 4: PROJECT MinE.

PROJECT MinE is a global collaboration with the goal to sequence the genomes of at least 15,000 people with ALS to

---

39   http://www.alsa.org/news/archive/funding-neuro-collaborative.html

discover new genes that affect ALS risk. Discovering these variants and understanding how they contribute to disease—or protect against it—is likely to lead to novel approaches to ALS therapies.

Each of these four initiatives include investigators from world class doctors/researchers/scientists mentioned previously in this book, including Jonathan Glass, MD, Emory University; Robert J. Brown, Jr. MD, University of Massachusetts; Merit Cudkowicz, MD, Massachusetts General Hospital; Clive Svendsen, PhD, Cedars-Sinai Medical Center; Donald Cleveland, PhD, University of California, San Diego; Steve Finkbeiner. MD, PhD, Gladstone Institute, University of California, San Francisco.

As renowned as these doctors, researchers, and scientists are, each of them also has their own individual ALS projects in which they have been deeply involved; for example, Dr. Jonathan Glass with Neuralstem; Dr. Robert Brown with genetics and now Brainstorm; Dr. Merit Cudkowicz with NEALS and now BrainStorm; and others.

Therefore, in order to greatly enhance and expedite the development of these four important initiatives, I propose each one should also be staffed with a full-time independent, unaffiliated, world-class researcher to assist and coordinate the efforts of these mostly part-time investigators in each of the four initiatives.

Additionally, according to Valerie Estess, director of research for Project A.L.S., a new and exciting ongoing research project involving genetics and the eyes of ALS patients is currently underway. Why do the muscles of the eyes remain functional with ALS patients, when most other muscles in the body begin to fail? The answer to that vital question could lead to a possible cure in itself! Therefore another independent, unaffiliated, world-class researcher also needs to be added to their staff for the reasons mentioned previously.

In the final analysis, once these initiatives are underway, these independent researchers of each initiative would share and coordinate their findings with both the director of research of the lead ALS organization and the new head and chief ALS researcher to be hired and appointed by the board of directors of the proposed new division. In this manner, this ALS research, along with all ALS research implemented under the new Billion Dollar Plan, would be coordinated under this one central umbrella.

These additional world-class researchers would be funded by the "Billion Dollar Plan" as described and proposed in the previous chapter of this book.

In addition to the few great minds listed herein that are already focused on this killer, there are a number of other brilliant minds—scientists and researchers in this country, Great Britain, Israel, and elsewhere—that need to be found and brought into the search for a cure, or at the very least initially turning ALS into a chronic disease rather than a fatal one.

We need to go after more of the best of the best, the most brilliant of the brilliant, with big salaries and huge incentives, including furnishing them with whatever laboratories, equipment, and assistants they require to overcome all obstacles and move forward to conquer this dreaded disease. There is a plethora of the most brilliant scientists spending their time researching cures for major diseases. So search them out, select the absolute best of those minds, make them an offer they can't refuse, including incentives, and bring them into the fight against ALS. Remember the American and British code breakers of World War II, who broke the secret military codes of Germany and Japan and significantly contributed to winning that great battle against tyranny? Well, this is another code to be broken—one of nature, and one of urgency!

These important new initiatives of the ALS Association and Project A.L.S. should mark the *"End of the Beginning"* to find a cure for ALS. My "Billion Dollar Plan," which could launch *far more new initiatives and expedite them all* by collaborating with pharmaceutical companies both large and small and offering them major incentives toward finding a cure, would be the *"Beginning of the End"* to eradicate ALS!

"Old Blood and Guts," four-star General George S. Patton, once said when addressing his troops, "No bastard ever won a war by dying for his country. He won it by making the other poor dumb bastard die for his country." What we want and need to do is to make that ALS "son of a bitch" die for its country, wherever it exists!

A BILLION FOR BRILLIANCE

This is akin to the NFL and MLB, where they pay millions upon millions of dollars to bring in the best coaches, quarterbacks, running backs, linemen, pitchers, fielders and hitters to WIN in their divisions and leagues, and take them to the Super Bowl and the World Series. The same approach needs to be made to "Strike Out" ALS, and NOW! A Billion for Brilliance! There is no time to waste, not one minute to spare!

Then major pharmaceutical companies, *with incentive grants from this new Research Division,* would take note of the work of these key scientists and researchers and back the human trials needed to prove both safety and efficacy for prompt FDA approval.

During the Civil War, in the Battle of Mobile Bay, Union Rear Admiral David G. Farragut asked why one of his ships was not moving ahead. When the reply came back that torpedoes were in her path, he boldly ordered, "Damn the torpedoes, full speed ahead!"

He and his fleet won that battle! So I say, "Damn the obstacles, full steam ahead!"

In basketball terms, what is needed is an aggressive "full-court press," and never, ever let up until the mission of defeating ALS is totally accomplished.

CONCLUSION: HEED THE FINAL WORDS OF FDR

The day President Franklin Delano Roosevelt (FDR) died, he was in the Little White House at Warm Springs, Georgia, preparing an address he was to deliver the next day, Jefferson Day, on April 13, 1945. The final words he wrote before his pen dropped from his hand were recorded for posterity and are as follows:

> The only limits to our realization of tomorrow
> Will be our doubts of today. Let us move
> forward with strong and active faith.

There is nothing impossible to accomplish in this great nation of ours—"the land of the free and the home of the brave." Look at what's been achieved in the last century alone; discovering penicillin and later more potent antibiotics that have saved the lives of millions; finding a cure for polio; the Manhattan Project and the splitting of the atom that was used to make the first atomic bomb, which ended WWII; and remember Neil Armstrong's words, "One small step for man, one great leap for mankind" as he set foot upon the Moon. May we never forget that the last four letters of the word "American" spell "I CAN!"

EPILOGUE

Regarding the possibility of accomplishing the "impossible," on the final page of my last book about tolerance, *A House of David in the Land of Jesus,* there is a prayer worth repeating here:

A Franciscan Benediction
May God bless you with discomfort,
at easy answers, half-truths, and superficial relationships, so that
you may live deep within your heart.

May God bless you with anger,
at injustice, oppression, and exploitation of people, so that you
may work for justice, freedom, and peace.

May God bless you with tears,
To shed for those who suffer from pain, rejection, starvation,
and war, so that you may reach out your hand to comfort them
and turn their pain to joy.

And may God bless you with enough foolishness,
to believe that "you can make a difference" in this world, so
that you can do what others claim cannot be done.
—Amen and amen.

"Someday we'll name a cure after Lou Gehrig,
instead of a disease."

—ALS Association, Golden West Chapter

There are ample other stories I could have told in this book, but these are some of the most memorable and significant ones that have transpired thus far during my days on this earth. I only wish that the reader has enjoyed them as much as I have relished telling them, and even more importantly, I hope that some who think that one or more of these Final Four humanitarian projects have merit will devote their time and resources to carrying them forward toward a successful conclusion.

ABOUT THE AUTHOR

Robert Lewis Berman was born in Atlanta, Georgia, in 1931 to Fay and Joe Berman, who was a member of the Atlanta City Council. At the age of five, Bob moved with his family to Lexington, Mississippi, after his grandmother, Julia Lewis, wife of Morris Lewis Sr., was killed in an automobile accident.

At the age of ten, just prior to the beginning of World War II, Bob and his family went back to Atlanta, where his father was stationed at Central Army Command. When his father went overseas to the Pacific Theater, they returned to Lexington, where he attended high school.

At the University of Mississippi, Bob was president of the Phi Eta Sigma honorary scholastic society; a member of the Omicron Delta Kappa (ODK) leadership society, the Phi Epsilon Pi social fraternity, and the Delta Sigma Pi business fraternity; co-chair of Religious Emphasis Week; vice president of the student body, and president of the campus senate; and, during his senior year, one of six members selected to the Hall of Fame.

After graduating with a BBA degree, Bob served as a First Lieutenant in the U.S. Army's 10th Infantry Division as a platoon leader, and as company executive officer of a rifle company.

Upon his honorable discharge, he attended the Harvard Business School where he received an MBA. It was there he met his future wife, Sondra "Sondy" Shindell, from New Haven, Connecticut. She was a senior at Lesley College in Cambridge, where she graduated cum laude, and a student at the New England

Conservatory of Music in Boston. They were married after graduation in 1957 and have happily shared their life together for the past fifty-eight years. They have three married daughters and seven grandchildren: Marjie and attorney husband Mark Block reside with their three sons, Jordan, Joshua, and Jared, in Manhattan Beach, California; Debbie and her real estate-developer husband Larry Silver reside with their son, Spencer, and daughter, Madison, in Delray Beach, Florida; Sheri and her attorney husband Steven Spector reside with their daughter, Megan, and son, Cole, in San Diego, California.

During his long business career, Bob has been chairman and president of Southern Food Brokerage, a sales and marketing food brokerage company; president of Berman Enterprises; a real estate broker and developer; and an author. Additionally he developed two restaurants, one Chinese and the other Italian.

He is past president of Beth Israel Congregation in Jackson, Mississippi; past president of the 350-member Rotary Club of Jackson; and past district governor of Rotary International. He has also served on a number of other boards of directors.

Bob and his wife have a primary residence in Boca Raton, Florida, and also reside part time in Los Angeles, California.

Chasing Rainbows and Beyond is his third nonfiction book.

This Book Belongs To Clinton Payne

From his Daughter, Carla 6.18.16